D0375745

THE
Life
AND
Death
DILEMMA

Other Books by Joni Eareckson Tada

All God's Children with Gene Newman
Choices . . . Changes
Diamonds in the Dust
Joni
A Step Further

NOW WITH DISCUSSION QUESTIONS

THE
Life
AND
Death
DILEMMA

A Revised Edition of *When Is It Right to Die?*

Families Facing Health Care Choices

Joni Eareckson Tada

ZondervanPublishingHouse
Grand Rapids, Michigan

A Division of HarperCollins*Publishers*

The Life and Death Dilemma
Families Facing Health Care Choices
Copyright © 1992, 1995 by Joni Eareckson Tada

Requests for information should be addressed to:
Zondervan Publishing House
Grand Rapids, Michigan 49530

Editorial Assistant: Steve Jensen

Library of Congress Cataloging-in-Publication Data

Tada, Joni Eareckson.
     The life and death dilemma: families facing health care choices/ Joni
Eareckson Tada.
         p.   cm.
     Originally published under title: When is it right to die?
     Includes bibliographical references.
     ISBN: 0-310-58571-6 (softcover)
         1. Suicide—Social aspects—United States.   2. Suicide—Religious
     aspects—Christianity.   3. Euthanasia—Social aspects—United States.
     4. Euthanasia—Religious aspects—Christianity.   5.   Right to die—United
     States.   6.   Handicapped—United States—Attitudes.   I. Title.
     [HV6548.U5T33   1994]
     362.2'8'0973—dc20   94-48419
                                                                    CIP

Edited by Mary McCormick
Interior design by Sherri L. Hoffman

Printed in the United States of America.

95 96 97 98 99 00 /❖ DH/ 10 9 8 7 6 5 4 3 2 1

*In memory of
Dan Piantine,
who now clings to heaven's prize
and breathes holy air.*

CONTENTS

Foreword   8

Special Thanks   9

PART ONE: Facing the Dilemma
  1. There Are Answers   13
  2. What Are the Questions?   29
  3. God Sets the Standards   51

PART TWO: Does It Matter?
  4. Your Decision Matters to Others   69
  5. Your Decision Matters to You   85
  6. Your Decision Matters to the Enemy   99
  7. Your Decision Matters to God   113

PART THREE: You Can Have the Mind of Christ
  8. It's Time to Decide   133
  9. Ending Well   157
  10. Living Victoriously   175

Notes   187

FOREWORD

Joni Eareckson Tada has written a timely, fresh discussion that speaks with a balanced voice to the question: When is it right to die? Not only does she address an issue being forced upon us as individuals, but one that has been suggested for a societal decision.

Joni speaks with a voice of one who has been there, who *is* there. She has known the uncertainty, the fear, the overwhelming truth, the despair, and the unendingness of a permanent disability. She has considered the options, discusses them openly from the heart, and shares with us her considered judgment. Those of us who are not in Joni's wheelchair may never be able to see the issues through Joni's eyes, but after reading this book we will see them more clearly than ever before.

Joni provides strong Christian, biblical arguments regarding euthanasia. But if you are not inclined to those authorities, remember that even though our society worships at the altar of high technology and seeks control of nature, the conquest of death will always elude us. Nevertheless, control over death is ever tempting.

Let those who seek death with dignity beware, lest they lose life with dignity in the process.

C. Everett Koop, M.D.
Surgeon General USPHS (1981–89)

Special Thanks

On this page you're invited to join in on an awards banquet where you can have a seat at the head table and listen to the accolades. If you're interested, stay and watch the plaques of recognition handed out. Sit awhile and listen to the speeches. These people whom I'm about to recognize are pretty special.

Francie Lorey and Judy Butler. These two deserve the highest awards. They served as my hands in research and writing. They gave of their time, including Saturdays, and love to see this book completed.

Dr. John M. Frame. Only after I read his book *Medical Ethics: Principles, Persons, and Problems* was I convinced I could tackle the issue.

Dr. Nigel M. de S. Cameron of Trinity Evangelical Divinity School. His instruction and guidance in ethics guaranteed that this book would reflect sound judgment and solid morals.

David Neff, Managing Editor of *Christianity Today*. Whenever I wandered off the beaten path theologically or ethically, David was there to steer me back on course.

Dr. C. Everett Koop. Salt to our culture. Light to our nation. A prophet to the medical society, the legal establishment, the religious community, and to disabled persons and their families.

I want to thank Steve Jensen for assisting me with facelifting *When Is It Right To Die?* The new and revised edition truly is worthy of its new title, *The Life and Death Dilemma.* I credit Steve with all the researching and writing of the discussion questions at the end of each chapter.

John Sloan, my editor, and Scott Bolinder, my publisher. Thank you and the rest of my friends at Zondervan for giving focus, direction, and every resource needed to get the job done. Bless you for believing I have something to say. And yes, it's nice to be back with family again.

Michael and Georgie Lynch, along with the entire *JAF* staff. You helped keep things around the office going forward, even when my door was closed and the "Do Not Disturb" sign was hung out. Abundant thanks to the Monday lunch group for their constant encouragements.

My deepest appreciation goes to the people whose testimonies make up the backbone of this book. Their spirit has challenged me to face the moral judgments I must make with courage and conviction.

And the best for last—my husband, Ken.

PART ONE

Facing the Dilemma

1

There Are Answers

Any idiot can face a crisis; it's this day to day living that wears you out.

Anton Chekhov

Chekhov's words were no doubt intended to be a backhanded encouragement. They elicit a knowing smile from those of us facing the day-to-day struggles of modern life—mortgages, diapers, cranky bosses, sibling fights, aches, and pains. Such mundane troubles wear us out, and a crisis now and then can seem a welcome diversion.

But what would Chekhov say to people facing a crisis that had become day to day?

What would Chekhov say to people like Sharon:

My father had Parkinson's disease for many years. He became dangerous to himself and to my mother to the point that the doctor put him into the hospital for surgery for prostate problems and then into a nursing home. At that time we were told he also had Alzheimer's disease.

After four years of being in a coma (brought on by undetected diabetes), amputation of first a toe, then a leg, there would come the amputation of the other leg and both hands. He had been in a coma for months but showed extreme pain in his facial gestures. He had not recognized me for about four to five years. My father was a wonderful man, husband, poppa, and grandpa who was loved by all.

He was also a proud man and very self-sufficient. It was so sad to see his weakness take away every part of him except breath—due to feeding tubes and life support.

Sharon and her mom faced life-and-death questions on a daily basis for four years. "Do we continue treatments?" "Do we 'pull the plug'?" "Do we remove the feeding tube?" I wonder if Chekhov pictured such questions being answered by "any idiot."

And what would Chekhov say to people like Jim and Julie?

Julie endured eight surgeries and biopsies and four regimens of chemotherapy. We experienced the dread and terror of two years of watching Julie receive, and then react to, those powerful drugs …

She lost her hair three different times. She would get deathly sick. Her face would turn white, her eyes dark. Her fingernails became knurled and black. Her mouth and entire GI track would break out in open, bleeding ulcers. Her white blood-cell count was often below 1000. A common cold could have killed her. She underwent a full course of radiation and a six-week, risky bone-marrow transplant. At one point, she had hanging over her, thirteen IV bottles filled with powerful drugs and antibiotics. We also experi-

enced five unsuccessful trips out to the National Cancer Institute. Their state-of-the-art experiment failed.

Jim and Julie lived in a health care crisis for seven years before Julie went home to heaven. For them there was always the wondering: "Will this drug work?" "Is the cancer really gone?" "Do we try this risky experiment?" They faced these questions, all while raising four kids and serving in full-time ministry.

And what would Chekhov say to Debbie:

I am a mother of three beautiful triplet girls. They were born three months early, despite fourteen weeks of bed rest and medication to try to prevent premature delivery. As a result of their extreme prematurity, two of the girls are handicapped.

The girls are two years old now and I am having a hard time trying to make sure everyone gets what she needs. Amanda is a normal two-year-old; Jennifer cannot crawl, sit up, or walk but mentally seems to be about fifteen months; and Rachel can sit up and crawl but mentally seems to be ten–twelve months. Both Jennifer and Rachel do not eat and need g-tube feedings (feeding through a tube into the stomach) and medications around the clock besides physical therapy, occupational therapy, speech therapy, and feeding therapy. Everything I do is devoted to and revolves around them and their needs, but I still go to bed at night knowing how much better they could be if I could do more ...

Our church was great in the beginning, and people were always helping me, but as the girls showed evidence of lasting problems, the help stopped. The problem is that I need help now more than ever. I have had a nurse in the home twenty-four hours a day for two years, but they are cutting that down to nothing by Christmas because the girls are off oxygen and their ventilators ...

To top everything off, right now the girls are in a rehabilitation facility for three months for intense feeding therapy. They are miserable there, and I have had to put Amanda in day care so I can be there for Jen and Rachel. We have no family nearby to help with all this ...

Debbie is looking ahead to years of daily crises of disability with her kids. She and her husband will ask: "How will the kids get an education?" "Where will the money come from to pay for therapy?" "Are we ever going to get a break just for us?"

We Are in a Dilemma

Crises like the ones just described are being rehearsed everywhere. Twenty-eight years in a wheelchair has introduced me to the world of advocacy, and with it, thousands of people who were either sinking into or surfacing out of suicidal despair. Decades of visiting hospitals and rehab centers has introduced me to the business executive with Lou Gehrig's disease whose body was shrinking and shriveling; to the young athlete paralyzed from a spinal cord injury and living in a nursing home; to the Vietnam veteran coping with a strange new mental illness; and to the teenager with cerebral palsy sitting on the sidelines, watching her classmates date, and drive cars.

These crises are not private. While straining to cope with their own pain, people are learning that they are part of a confusing debate in society over medical issues ranging from physician-assisted suicide to rationed health care. Along with advocates on both sides of the issue, they are learning technical distinctions between words like *nonvoluntary euthanasia* and *active euthanasia*. Technological advances in how we can treat people and keep them alive have added to the confusion surrounding the debate.

The pain and confusion expressed by people in crisis has made it fashionable (and compassionate according to some) to talk about a simple yet deadly solution: "Give it up. It's not worth the pain."

The result has fueled dangerous trends: Several states have placed death-and-dying issues on the ballot. Assisted suicide is now promoted and practiced as a right. The Hemlock Society, a pro-euthanasia organization, is growing in membership and in its promotion. The unthinkable is now being argued on talk shows.

Having observed the pain experienced by people and having participated in the public debate on issues such as euthanasia and health care, I am convinced that the crisis has become the norm for our society. *We face a collective dilemma in society regarding the decisions we make about death, health, and disability.* The dilemma encompasses every area of our lives. People have been pushed to make decisions they never imagined they would make. And we are losing them in the process. The answer to Dr. Francis Shaeffer's and Dr. C. Everett Koop's question *Whatever Happened To The Human Race?* is: "We're killing ourselves."

There Is Time

I know you care about this societal crisis, but right now you want to solve your own personal crisis. Decisions and tensions are being thrust upon you at every turn. The hospital room has replaced the family room. Free time is measured in minutes, not weekends. Fatigue becomes the norm, and sleep, if you get any, is your only solace. And just once you would like to see a day's pile of mail that does not contain an envelope from a doctor or pharmacy.

Jesus knew people like you, people in daily crises. He lived for three years among people imprisoned in physical, emotional, and spiritual trauma that alienated them from society. And though the gospels recount numerous dealings Jesus had with such people, there is one man's story that catches my attention.

The man in crisis was Bartemeus. He was blind, broke, and broken. He had no way to make a living except by being an obnoxious beggar. So Bartemeus, upon hearing the crowd and Jesus approach Jericho, called out in his need.

You can predict correctly that Jesus healed Bartemeus and relieved him of the crisis. But listen carefully to two words in the narrative account. Before any crisis was resolved for Bartemeus, it says that "Jesus stopped."[1]

Jesus stopped. In the midst of a crowd of people who knew no crises—people who were wrapped up in day-today living—Jesus stopped for a man who had known nothing but crisis. Picture Jesus on his way to his ultimate mission of redemption, pressed in on all sides by people who were expecting him to be their king. In the midst of that chaotic mob scene, Jesus stopped once again as he had done hundreds of times before, to talk to one man in crisis.

May I do the same with you? May I wheel up beside you in these pages and stop to talk? To listen? To engage your heart in what God has to say about your crisis? About the decisions you are having to make?

About you?

I am inviting myself to do so because I have also been a participant in prolonged crises and have found that living in the Refiner's fire has been all that it is publicized to be—purposeful and painful. A diving accident as a teenager left me paralyzed from the shoulders down. Issues of life and death became all-consuming. During those days, my depression wasn't mild or fleeting. I was gripped with the dull, lonely ache of despair. My personal holocaust is described in the book *Joni*:

> Here I was, trapped in this canvas cocoon. I couldn't move anything except my head. Physically, I was little more than a corpse. I had no hope of ever walking again. I could never lead a normal life and marry Dick. *In fact, he might even be walking out of my life forever*, I concluded. I had absolutely no idea of how I could find purpose or meaning in just existing day after day—waking, eating, watching TV, sleeping.

Why on earth should a person be forced to live out such a dreary existence? How I prayed for some accident or miracle to kill me. The mental and spiritual anguish was as unbearable as the physical torture.

(December 1967, from the book, *Joni*)[2]

My family has become all too familiar with health crises. We have watched a cancerous tumor destroy my five-year-old niece's brain until she withered and died. My sister had to face the daily crisis of comforting her daughter, seeking answers from doctors, hoping for healing—all while facing the loss of her husband in a divorce. Health care decisions were emotional. Had it not been for the child's sweet hope of heaven, it would have been unbearable for us.

And most recently, my father, before going to heaven, ushered us into the web of life-and-death decisions. His last days gave us a crash course in family decision making, and we were on our knees often.

There Is Wisdom

Who would have ever dreamed of the day when a family of a dying loved one would have to study a medical dictionary to discern exactly what "dying" is? And did we wonder at the altar on our wedding day if "better or worse, richer or poorer" was meant to include a spouse in a permanent vegetative state with medical bills in the hundreds of thousands of dollars? Idiots in a crisis? Hah! You feel like you've earned an M.D. and a Ph.D.!

And just when you think you have worked out a system for making decisions, someone raises questions regarding value and quality of life. Is it worth the money to apply this procedure? Will the patient ever be useful in life again? Will the family be able to handle the stress this decision will entail?

The questions seem impossible. How could there be any answers? How am I supposed to know what to do?

You don't. But God does. God is not the author of confusion regarding the choices you are being asked to make. I am convinced from observing His character and reading His promises that even the most perplexing dilemmas, or even the highest-priced technological advances, are not beyond Him.

Take courage in this thought: If God has given man tools with which to sustain life, it would seem impossible to outrun His wisdom. God, by nature, can't say, "Well, people, I don't know what to do about those machines and treatments you've invented. And your arguments and legal terms are too sophisticated for my universe. You'll have to make those decisions in your realm because I can't comprehend it all, much less offer wisdom."

God doesn't operate that way. If He provides man with the talent to advance and invent for the sake of life, He must also provide the wisdom to make decisions for the sake of good.

I am convinced of that logic because of what God has promised. In Christ, he says, ". . . are hidden all the treasures of wisdom and knowledge."[3] And consider Daniel's observation after God gave him needed wisdom on the eve of his crisis: "He gives wisdom to the wise and knowledge to the discerning."[4]

If you feel you can't identify with a spiritual heavy-weight like Daniel, remember that God's wisdom is within reach. "If *any* of you lacks wisdom, he should ask God, who gives generously to *all* without finding fault, and it will be given to him."[5]

The Bible tells us that there is only one prerequisite God places on your search for wisdom during your prolonged crisis—namely, that you fear God. "Who, then, is the man that fears the Lord? He will instruct him in the way chosen for Him,"[6] and "The fear of the Lord is the beginning of wisdom."[7]

The attitude of reverence and acknowledgment of His authority and power must be present with you in every circumstance—at the death bed, in the waiting room, and in the nursing home. At every point of decision and every expression of hope, we must acknowledge His sovereign will. God is the giver and sustainer of all life, and He is holy. Our dependence upon Him for wisdom must be accompanied by the knowledge that we are accountable to him for how we apply that wisdom. We must defer to Him in all our decisions. When He shows us something through wisdom and His word, we have to agree not to second-guess, manipulate, or misconstrue.

There Is Peace

Wisdom from God is a package deal. It is not dispensed without an accompanying gift. In God's grace he gives peace as well as wisdom. How cruel it would be if it were not so. For if God dispensed wisdom without peace, we would be tempted to ignore it at the first sign of trouble. Without the inward assurance that God gave us wisdom, our path would be diverted by every doctor, lawyer, TV commentator, and well-meaning friend. "Wisdom that comes from heaven is first of all pure; then peace-loving . . ."[8]

A funny thing about this peace: While the wisdom from God is clear and discernable, the peace is not. It is beyond our understanding, as Paul told the Philippians. It is the kind of peace that will be inexplicable to the doctors and nurses who watch you deal with the crisis. You might even be accused at times by people of being "in denial." "She's just avoiding the issue," they might say. "If he really knew what was going on and what his decision would mean, he wouldn't act so calm."

Peace from God is not denial. It appears that way because you are being guarded. God's peace, Paul says, "will guard your hearts and your minds in Christ Jesus."[9] Notice what is being guarded—both your heart and your mind. Your attitudes, your emotions, your thoughts, your decisions—all are being guarded when covered by the peace of God!

There Is Strength

Wisdom and peace speak to the inner needs of our mind and heart. They give us heavenly stature in the midst of prolonged crises that the world doesn't understand.

"But what about my body? Give me a one-way ticket to Tahiti 'cause I'm fed up with this!"

I know the feeling. Some days I just want to quit. "Forget it, God. There's no point in dragging this immobile body out of bed. Turn off the lights. Turn off the brain. I'm outta' here!"

Our earthly flesh constantly wars against the spirit. When it is healthy, our bodies seek to be satisfied with pleasures. When it is fatigued, it seeks to be delivered by fleeing the circumstance or even life itself.

God's grace is not immune to the needs of our flesh. Strength, like wisdom and peace, are appropriated to us in measures that meet the need of the hour. My friend with post-polio, Shirley Locker, writes about such daily grace in her tract "It's So Daily."

> A friend of mine and I were discussing some of the problems connected with our disabilities, and she summed it up by saying, "The main problem with a physical handicap is that it's so daily!" I couldn't agree with her more.
>
> The daily struggle with disability is different from the discomfort of a cold or the pain of recovering from surgery or a broken leg. Health problems like these are usually cured with the passing of time.
>
> Not so with a physical disability. We wake up every morning to the same set of circumstances. Even when we have learned to live with the disability and adjusted to the limitations, the daily struggle is still there ...
>
> But these same daily struggles have their own rewards for the ones who trust in God for their daily strength. God has promised in Deuteronomy 33:25 (kjv), "As thy days, so shall thy strength be."

... We can depend on His promise in 2 Corinthians 12, "My grace is sufficient for thee: my strength is made perfect in weakness."

Shirley Locker from *It's So Daily*[10]

Shirley writes as a quadriplegic who knows of the daily strength given by God. She will be the first to admit that she feels tired and weak and at times would like to simply stay in bed, but God's daily provision will not let her.

There Are Answers

I have spoken these words of encouragement to you now because you will need to be assured of God's wisdom, peace, and strength *before* you consider the questions raised in this book. You *can* make good choices. You *can* live at peace. You *can* make it through the day.

And I know that there are answers. Although my depression seemed as paralyzing as my spinal-cord injury, I had found an answer that made life worth living. Our family also found an answer for my suffering, cancer-ridden niece. And perhaps, most poignant, there was even a touching answer for my dying father.

I am convinced that the same principles that guided me and my family through the nightmarish maze of depression, suicide, and death can help others. What we have learned as a family can benefit other hurting families. And that's the reason for the book you hold in your hands.

Perhaps you are the quadriplegic in a wheelchair or the young mother of a little girl dying of a degenerative nerve disease. You may be sitting at the bedside of an elderly parent who is sinking deeper and deeper into dementia. Or maybe, just maybe, your life does not even touch the world of the terminally ill or dying or disabled. You are just plain tired of living, for whatever painful reason. Your problems have piled up so high they only wear you down. Pain has become numbing. Your thinking has become clouded. You are tired, so very tired. Quiet desperation has settled in, and you couldn't care less if there are answers.

There is hope. And though you are in a crisis, you are not an idiot. An answer that you can live with is within reach. This book is not about systems of ethics but about people like you and me and the judgments we must make.

Discussion Guide

What Would You Do?

You may not feel prepared for this, but let's jump right into the heat of the battle and wrestle with a hypothetical situation that is actually quite a common experience. So many of the principles you need to make a decision have not yet been covered in the book, but this will help you get a feel for the sense of dilemma that people face. Dilemmas aren't easy, nor do the participants feel as though they have all the facts. Read the following scenario and decide what you would do in the circumstance described.

A 78-year-old woman named Charlotte, who is a Christian, has Alzheimer's disease and has been placed by her family in a nursing home. She has severe dementia and does not recognize her friends or family members. Charlotte is becoming increasingly agitated. She is not able to feed herself adequately and doctors have suggested to her family that a feeding tube be inserted to ensure that she receive proper nutrition. The family is divided on this question; Charlotte never made clear her wants and wishes about life supports. Charlotte's daughter wants to say yes to the feeding tube; her son insists no.

1. Before considering your advice, try to picture what the people in the story might be thinking or feeling.

What impact do you think this situation is having on them?

The daughter—

The son—

The doctor—

The nursing-home staff—

Charlotte—

2. If you were the decision maker, what would you do and why?

    Side with the son?

    Side with the daughter?

3. Is there any way to resolve the matter other than by siding with one or the other of Charlotte's children?

4. Assume that you are close to everyone in the family. Apart from the decision you made and the reasons for it, what would you tell them?

    Is there anything you would *do* for the family?

After you complete this book, come back to this discussion section and answer the questions again. Do you notice any difference in your answers? Discuss your decisions again and share your differences.

2

WHAT ARE THE QUESTIONS?

If God has answers, what are the questions?

That sounds like a flippant remark you'd find on a bumper sticker, but it's actually a legitimate question for us to consider here. Making godly decisions in the life-and-death dilemma require a clear understanding of the issues. Just what is it you are having to decide? What are the options? What are the consequences?

The purpose of this chapter is to clarify and define the three major life-and-death dilemmas being faced by people today. This chapter also examines the choices people are making and the reasons for their choices. Defining terms and articulating the questions will equip you to be a better decision maker. And understanding how society is responding to the life-and-death dilemma will guard you from making the same faulty choices.

The life-and-death dilemma is divided into three categories: death, health, and disability. Though different in many respects, each of these subjects deals with similar problems and decision-making criteria.

The Dilemma of Dying

Death is not as straightforward as it used to be. Do you remember seeing old films in which a mirror was placed under a person's nose? If the mirror fogged up, the person was alive. If not, the person was dead. Plain and simple. And we all wish, at times, that dying were as easy to read as, "Naked I came from my mother's womb, and naked I will depart. The Lord gave and the Lord has taken away."[1] We long for the days of cut-and-dried, black-and-white, yes-or-no answers. But technology has changed all of that. Doctors can identify different stages of death. We also have the capability of controlling the onset and pace of the dying process. That control has brought with it a new vocabulary.

Medically speaking, death is an event in which there is irreversible cessation of total brain function. This includes all three levels of brain function: the cerebral cortex, which houses our higher-order thinking and functioning; the middle brain; and the brain stem, which controls body functions such as breathing and heart rate.

Simple concepts so far. The dilemma begins, however, when we talk about the various states of consciousness of a person and the time frame in which death might occur.

Persistent vegetative state or *permanent loss of consciousness* describes a person whose cerebral cortex, that part of the brain responsible for higher thought and motor functions, is said by many to be destroyed, but the brain stem, that part of the brain that keeps the heart and lungs functioning, is still alive.

Mid-brain death or "locked-in" syndrome describes a person who is able to carry out the life functions of heart and lungs. In addition, he or she might be able to communicate through crude means such as blinking the eyes. The person will be aware of his or her surroundings but not able to act upon the surroundings.

Coma is a general term used to describe unconsciousness. Comas may last for a short period of time or extend for a lifetime. It is distinguished from the previous two states because no death of any portion of the brain may have occurred.

The life-and-death dilemma is not limited to situations in which a person is unconscious. It also involves those who are terminally ill and those who are "imminently dying."

Terminal illness is generally applied to someone who is conscious but who will, in all likelihood, die within six months. A person with inoperable and untreatable cancer or a person in the last stages of AIDS might fall under this category if determined by doctors to have less than six months to live without hope of a cure or an extension.

Imminently dying is used to describe a person who rapidly and irreversibly deteriorates in his or her condition and who will most likely die within hours or days. Vital functions, such as that of the kidneys, begin shutting down. Intervention will not stop death but will simply prolong the dying process.

All of the preceding medical conditions have one thing in common: the potential for someone—the patient, the family, the doctors, or the state—to intervene in some way to either accelerate or delay death. Such intervention can come in the form of withholding or interjecting treatment to hasten, cause, or allow death.

Euthanasia is supposed to signify "good death," but today's meaning of the word is confusing because it conjures up images of everything from pulling the plug on a dying loved one to the killing of millions in Nazi Germany who were considered socially unuseful. Practically speaking, euthanasia means to produce death or assist an individual in achieving death because others, or even the patient himself, consider life no longer worth living. The motive is usually to relieve suffering, save money, or do away with the indignities associated with dying. Under this broad definition fall a few more specific terms.

Voluntary euthanasia is to cause death with the person's approval and consent. Jamie Lou Martin was in a car accident that left her paralyzed from the lips down and in excruciating pain in the hospital. She cried out to be relieved of her life. Gary Weidner, a next-door neighbor, responded to Jamie's request by killing her and then attempting to kill himself. Though sentenced to fifteen years in prison, two appellate judges amended the sentence to the time served, with a period of probation.

Nonvoluntary euthanasia is to cause death without a person's consent through approval secured from a family member, hospital panel, or court. The key is that the patient is incompetent, and someone else must decide either what the patient would have wanted or what is in his best interests. Claire Conroy, eighty-four, was under a nephew's guardianship. She suffered from multiple ailments. She was not in a coma nor brain-dead when the nephew requested that her feeding tube be removed in order to hasten death. Claire died of natural causes before the court made its decision.

Passive euthanasia is mercy killing by withholding or withdrawing medical treatment such as food and water. Clarence Herbert, a fifty-five-year old man, suffered brain damage while undergoing heart surgery. His family had his respirator removed, with the expectation that he would die. He did not and so was denied food and water. He died six days later. An appellate court dropped murder charges against the physicians, ruling that artificial administration of food and water (through a tube) constituted medical treatment.

Assisted suicide occurs when a physician or family member aids a person toward death. Janet Adkins, a woman with Alzheimer's disease, took this approach when she and her husband drove to Michigan to enlist the services of Jack Kevorkian. Kevorkian set up the equipment so that Janet could handle the necessary tubes to give herself a lethal injection to stop her heart.

The definitions are being practiced in sometimes gruesome ways, aren't they? The courts and various state legislatures are also dealing with these definitions on a regular basis. As of this writing, New York, California, and Florida face suits from people seeking to declare that laws against assisted suicide violate the Fourteenth Amendment of the U.S. Constitution. A New Jersey father is seeking the right to commit suicide so that his family will not be discriminated against by the insurance company that carries his life insurance. And Michigan is currently engaged in three court cases regarding assisted suicide.

With these definitions as a backdrop, let's consider the questions facing individuals and their families in the dilemma of dying.

Do I place my family member on life support even though he may never regain consciousness? The doctor tells me only his brain stem is alive. What do I do?

Do I take my family member off life support? He can't go on living with tubes sticking out of him. And the doctors say there is no guarantee he will regain consciousness.

Should we authorize a feeding tube for our father because he can't eat on his own?

Should I have the doctors remove the feeding tube from my wife? She doesn't seem to be improving in her health and just lies there.

Should we ask that life-saving surgery be performed on my mom who is in a "locked-in" state?

Can I find a way to end my life? The pain and the depression are just more than I can handle. I'm going to die soon, anyway.

Isn't there someone who can put my brother out of his misery? I know that if he could speak, he would want someone to end his life for him.

These are the kinds of questions for which God has promised answers. Unfortunately, the manner in which many people are answering the questions today has taken on alarming characteristics.

The Dilemma of Health

Not everyone facing a life-and-death dilemma is dying or near death. Thousands of people are engaged in a conscious fight against disease and injury. Cures and treatments are pursued in a variety of ways and at varying costs. Each step carries with it either a sense of hope or a sense of utter despair. People linger between the land of the "normal and routine" and the land of the dying.

Health is a simpler term to describe. Health is typically understood to be a condition whereby vital functions are normal and no medical intervention is necessary either for procuring or for sustaining the body's typical activity.

Though the issue seems straightforward (everyone wants health), individuals and families still find themselves in severe dilemmas. The story of Jim and Julie cited earlier in this book is an excellent illustration. They faced a host of options on how to treat the cancer. Within the boundaries of traditional medicine, they were able to pursue a variety of treatments for cancer. At the same time, they faced the constant barrage of advice on nontraditional treatments for cancer.

The dilemma of health is made even more complex when one considers the situation of the patient. The pursuit of health might be questioned in the case of a ninety-four-year-old diabetic but unquestioned if it were a nineteen-year-old co-ed. Or the potential for increased suffering with little improvement might make an otherwise good decision a bad one.

And are you ready for one more factor adding to the dilemma of health? Money. That's right. Health costs money. And people are being forced to make health care choices based on the availability of, or lack of, money. The money factor is such a complex and stressful part of the dilemma of health, in fact, that the entire country is engaged in heated debate over the issue.

Questions needing answers in light of the dilemma of health include:

Do we try this radical surgery or treatment?
Can we afford the treatment and subsequent cost of medicines?
Is the pain worth the results?
Will my life be improved as a result of this treatment?

Questions such as these are seeking answers in hospital rooms and in nursing homes on a regular basis.

The Dilemma of Disability

No one chooses to become disabled, but there are choices surrounding disability that create dilemmas similar in nature to those caused by death or health care. Issues regarding value of life, cost, pain and suffering, and ethics might all play a part in the dilemma of disability.

Disability in many cases, may not be an illness or a disease, but an incapacitating injury. Often disabling conditions occupy the same arena of decision making, namely the medical and rehabilitation field. Disabled people and their family members will often find themselves in doctors' and therapists' offices and filling out as many, if not more, forms than those who are sick or dying.

Though a person with a disability may outlive any comatose or sick person, the effects on the person and the family can be equally devastating. Suicide, divorce, and drug-abuse statistics among people with disabilities are high. "Disabled people all over the country have killed themselves," according to the World Institute on Disability. "… they see no hope, no future."[2]

What is this thing called "disability," which affects 540 million people worldwide in these ways? According to the Americans with Disabilities Act, disability is "a physical or mental impairment which limits one or more of the major life activities."[3] A person with muscular dystrophy or a person with Down's syndrome are examples of people with disabilities.

Disability has its own unique questions. Disabled people and their families wonder:

> *Should I put my aging parent in a nursing home or care for him myself?*
> *Should I divorce my husband, who is brain injured?*
> *Should I send my child to a special boarding school or keep her at home and try to mainstream her in a regular school?*
> *How can I find someone to give my husband and me a break from the routine?*
> *I can't face the pain of my disability anymore. How can I end my life? I am too disabled to do it myself. Can I ask someone to help me?*

These and other questions are seeking answers in the disability community. Some of the answers have meant hope for thousands, while some have been deadly.

Society's Answers

Having examined the questions, there is one more "bumper sticker" issue to address. If God has answers, why is no one listening?

Consider the following:

> *Final Exit*, a self-help guide to suicide, becomes a best-seller.
>
> Dr. Death, Jack Kevorkian, acquitted of charges stemming from his aiding his "patients" with a suicide machine.
>
> Jocelyn Elders, former Surgeon General, lauds effects of abortion on children with Down's syndrome.
>
> Holland turns blind eye to euthanasia.
>
> States place euthanasia and physician-assisted suicide on the legislative agenda.

These headlines tell me society has already begun to answer the questions without God's perspective. And the answers reflect a decline in the moral discipline of our society and a lost sense of human value. The answers look nothing like those with which you and I grew up. Those to whom we might have gone to for advice and leadership regarding our dilemma have passed from the scene. Consider the implications of what Jocelyn Elders, the nation's former Surgeon General, has said about the value of those with Down's syndrome:

Abortion has had an important, positive, public health effect. Many families at high risk of genetic defects are willing to become pregnant only because of the option of abortion. The number of Down's syndrome infants in Washington state in 1976 was sixty-four percent lower than it would have been without legal abortion.[4]

What Dr. Elders is saying is that people can and should consider choosing not to have children with Down's syndrome and that abortion is a legitimate means of fulfilling that desire. The underlying philosophy of such an attitude is not lost on the general public. Dr. Koop, another former surgeon general, with quite a different perspective from that of Dr. Elders, observed this:

> When I was doing research for the book and film, *Whatever Happened to the Human Race?*, I went to nursing homes and talked to people who felt that pressure. Old people were apologizing to me for using a bed, for being alive, for taking medication because they knew somebody else deserved it more.[5]

The fact that elderly people feel that way about themselves says something about the way society is handling the life-and-death dilemma. Society is making judgment calls and finding some of its citizens wanting.

Why?

What reason could anyone give for answering the life-and-death dilemma with a book like *Final Exit* or a suicide machine like Jack Kevorkian's? How could

Jocelyn Elders say what she did? Why are people taking their life or abandoning their loved ones?

These are not rhetorical questions to which there are no answers. People *do* have reasons, and they are more than willing to share them, especially when they are asked the question, "When is it right to die?" The following are the reasons I've heard most often. I share them with you in order to help you make a godly decision in the midst of your dilemma. Analyzing their reasons will help you to avoid being tempted to use the same reasons.

When Is It Right to Die?

It's None of Your Business

"You want a time? I'll give you a time," I could almost hear Arlene say. "It's when *you* decide. Period."

Arlene Randolph was athletic and full of life, but a fall during a hiking trip in the coastal mountains of California damaged her spinal cord. She became severely paralyzed. Doctors kept telling her that her life would brighten as soon as she could learn to sit up ... as soon as she could get a better wheelchair ... as soon as she could have a special-order bed ... as soon as she could go home. Life for Arlene didn't happen that neatly or cleanly. As her husband Phil put it, "Everything that could go wrong went wrong for her."

A self-directed young woman, Arlene knew whose life it was—her own. It wasn't her husband's and it wasn't her two children's. Her life was not owned by the doctors and nurses she left behind at the hospital. And the life-and-death choices she was contemplating certainly weren't the business of her rabbi or even the pastor who ran the little support group in her community.

Less than a year into her disability, Arlene made a decision. Unwilling to face a life without hands that worked or feet that walked, she decided to starve herself to death. Her husband stood with her and her decision. "She was set in her ways, and that's the way she's always been. And she was not depressed," her husband said.

I knew Arlene's disability was not a terminal illness, and she was far from death's door. She was, like me, disabled, and her decision was a deliberate suicide. Knowing about the physical pain that accompanies starvation, I sent her a letter. "Maybe our situations aren't exactly the same," I wrote, "but I can understand the loneliness, the confusion, the battle with resentment, and the many questions." As a fellow-disabled person, I pleaded with her to reconsider. But Arlene died not long after she received my letter.

I talked with Phil on the phone after his wife's death. "Do you wish Arlene would have waited a little longer before she decided to kill herself?"

There was silence on the other end and then a tentative "Yes. Yes. I think about it all the time." Then Phil was quick to add, "But it wasn't my choice to stop her. In fact, all of us, the whole family, supported her."

Arlene's death was her own business. That's what she believed. And even though pain management and provisions for independent living are better than ever for disabled people, things like customized wheelchairs, special-order beds, attendant care, adapted home environments, and financial aid are, to some people, the trees.

The forest is that they just don't want to live with a severely handicapping condition, and they believe the decision to die belongs to them alone.

I can't help but picture Arlene's life before her accident. It's easy to imagine her climbing the cliffs of Big Sur, blazing a trail into the wilderness, or powering ahead on her bicycle, leaving the pack in the dust. And in a way, her choice to die fits her do-it-yourself profile. After all, Arlene was obviously a first-class individual, a born-and-bred American who gripped onto her individualism as a highly prized value. Her brand of private initiative found its logical and ultimate expression in her decision to die. What's ironic is that in our society, which regards individualism as a valued tradition, Arlene's choice seems common, acceptable, and not surprising.

But was Arlene's demise her business and hers alone? To make a decision to die before life involuntarily leaves us is a decision we have the power to make. But is it possible such a choice is the ultimate expression of selfishness?

When Is It Right to Die?

When It's Too Expensive to Live

"Hey! For a lot of people, death is just plain cheaper than life!"

I never would have dreamed that would be the question on the minds of most people at a banquet attended by Christian health-care professionals. I was invited to present the main address, and the topic was "Assisted Suicide in the Disability Community." During the question-and-answer time, the concern turned to rising health-care costs. One doctor shook his head and said, "Costs for treatment are soaring beyond what anyone can handle. People are running up bills not covered by insurance or Medicare." He tapped his fingers on the table and added, "I think this whole life-and-death debate is going to be settled by economics."

I shivered. I couldn't help but think of the grandmother in a nursing home deciding to refuse treatment because her $10,000 a month care is eroding the college savings of her grandchildren. And I thought of the subtle pressure that society places on dying, terminally ill, or debilitated people, reminding them that expensive treatment does, after all, have its limits.

Are we to the point where health-care costs have forced us to put a different price tag on each person's life? What about those most economically vulnerable? A decision to forego treatment and face a quick death may be one of a few options for wealthy or well-insured persons, but a decision to cut life short may be the *only* option for people who are poor, abandoned, or severely debilitated.

When Is It Right to Die?

When Death Is Easier Than Facing Life

"There's a time when life is the foe and death is the friend."

A black moustache and beard. A black shirt. Black trousers, shoes, and socks. That was the first thing I noticed about Ken Bergstedt when his father wheeled him into my office, but our conversation was surprisingly lighthearted. While his father sat on the office sofa, Ken and I gabbed about our disabilities, how irked we were at wheelchair manufacturers that kept hiking prices, and how it was a good idea to always double-rinse the sheepskins we slept on. Our hour appointment passed quickly. Ken and his dad returned to their RV, and a day later headed back to their home in Las Vegas, Nevada.

After Ken left, I mused over our similarities and differences. We were old veterans when it came to our disabilities, but we were quite different when it came to our faith. My limitations had forged a stronger faith. His limitations had drained him of any spiritual notions. But I was grateful he kept in touch. I received a letter a couple of months later in which Ken included a few photos of how his dad had modified their RV for his wheelchair.

A year later I read about Ken in the newspaper. The article was cut-and-dried, explaining that Kenneth Bergstedt, a ventilator-dependent Nevada man, now wished his father to assist him in suicide. Ken's decision was exacerbated by the fear that his dad would soon pass away due to failing health. Both were afraid that Ken would not be adequately cared for once his dad died.

It was virtually impossible to get through to Ken once the news media got involved. Nevertheless, I tried to contact him, writing, "Is it true you said in an article that you have 'no happy or encouraging expectations to look for from life, and you live with constant fears and apprehensions'? Those words are chilling—they remind me of a time when I said the same. But don't have them pull you off the respirator."

I don't think my letter ever reached him. And from reading further accounts in the newspapers, it was clear why Ken wanted his father to kill him. Life seemed more frightening than death.

Four months later, I picked up the morning paper and saw a small notice on the bottom of the front page. Ken had died. His father died just a short time later.

The prospect of life without the familiarity of his dad's care was unbearable. Death, to Ken, appeared to be more of a friend than the known hell of life. The irony is, life without his father was yet to be lived; it didn't have to be hellish. I personally knew of people in his community who wanted to help him interpret the future as a friend, but Ken refused. What he knew of life appeared more ominous than what he knew of death.

Many would say that Kenneth Bergstedt from Las Vegas, Nevada, took a bigger gamble in choosing a black and uncertain oblivion instead of the brighter possibilities of life with potential for change.

When Is It Right to Die?

When Death Is a Matter of Mercy

"No decent human being would allow an animal to suffer without putting it out of its misery. It is only to human beings that human beings are so cruel as to allow them to live on in pain, in hopelessness, in living death, without moving a muscle to help them," said Isaac Asimov.[6]

Long ago I went to see a movie with my friends called *They Shoot Horses, Don't They?* I had just been discharged from the rehab center, and my friends thought it would be nice to enjoy some Friday night fun. Besides, the title had "horses" in it, so the movie couldn't be that bad, right?

Wrong. It was a story about a depressed person who wanted a friend to put a gun to her head to relieve her suffering. When the friend protested, Jane Fonda said with woeful eyes, "They shoot horses, don't they?" At that point we left the movie.

Art sometimes imitates life, and although the message of that movie may have been shocking when it was released twenty years ago, today more than sixty-three percent of Americans approve, in certain cases, of mercy killing.[7]

But what induces a person to cause a death and say, "This is for your own good"? Is it indeed because pain is excessive? Pain management is the most sophisticated and advanced as it's ever been. Is it living with limitations? Who knows what Arlene would have decided had she given her wheelchair a chance. Is it a suffering loved one's shattered dignity and loss of hope? Ah, are we motivated to mercy-kill because the loved one is hurting, or are we motivated by a confused sense of guilt and sympathy, suffering as we watch him?

"No decent human being would allow an animal to suffer without putting it out of its misery," said Mr. Asimov. Oddly, suffering animals aren't endowed with human characteristics such as dignity or hope, no matter how forcibly Isaac Asimov or movie makers may argue.

Mercy is defined as "kind or compassionate treatment."[8] Mr. Asimov chides people for not moving a muscle to help those who hurt. I heartily agree. But are there not better ways to demonstrate kindness and compassion than to send a loved one off into a black and uncertain oblivion?

Had Enough?

We have covered a great deal of ground and unearthed some disturbing issues.

Are you depressed or angry at how people are responding to the life-and-death dilemma? Good. That means you're open to seeking God's perspective.

Are you depressed or angry because you agree with some of the decisions and reasons that people are promoting? Please, don't let go. Give God a chance to speak His mind. It will be worth it.

Discussion Guide

Let's Define the Issues

People are defining the issues in the life-and-death dilemma on a daily basis. A good working knowledge of the issues being defined will help you to be a better decision maker yourself and also enable the church to speak to society at large.

1. Death is medically described as total brain death at which point there is permanent loss of all three levels of the brain. Do you think this is a good working definition? Why or why not?

2. This chapter listed several questions faced by individuals and families facing the life-and-death dilemma. Review those questions on pages 30, 31, 33. Are there other questions people might face in addition to these?

   Have you ever had to face the kinds of questions described? If so, share them with the group.

3. Consider the following answers to the question "When is it right to die?":

   "It's none of your business."

   "When it's too expensive to live."

   "When death is easier than facing life."

   "When death is a matter of mercy."

What would you say to the person citing the above answers? Remember, the person giving these reasons is not doing so for the sake of academic discussion. He or she is in severe pain and/or despair.

3

GOD SETS THE STANDARDS

Soldiers lay on the beach, pinned down under enemy fire. Some were alive. Most were dead. The invasion of Normandy had begun and along with it, the bloodbath that would make the whole enterprise seem like a cruel joke. It would take unusual displays of courage to turn the tide in favor of the Allies.

For one group of soldiers, it was their leader who displayed such courage. He shouted to his men, "There are two kinds of men on this beach. Those who are dead and those who are going to die!" And with that declaration of the obvious, he led a charge farther inland and away from the killing sands, saving scores of men and defeating the enemy.

Heroics of this kind were played out all along the coast of France in 1944. In each case, someone made a commitment to analyze a situation, declare an objective, and then lead. What interests me is not only the courage of the leaders but the courage of those who followed. Think about the soldier who has just heard the call or seen his platoon leader move ahead. Does he stay on the beach and take his chances? Does he move ahead as ordered? Talk about a life-and-death dilemma!

Which is why I share this illustration. In one sense you are pinned down under enemy fire in this crisis. You are facing a dilemma. You see casualties all around you—families breaking up, people losing their financial resources, and people giving up on God and on life. Some are opting for suicide. In the last chapter you read what some people are saying about why they are choosing to "stay on the beach." You recognize that their reasons are flawed or not pleasing to God in some way.

But despite such understanding, you may not feel helped in your dilemma. In fact you might feel all the more confused. The facts of your particular dilemma offer few clues, and no one piece of advice seems to move you in either direction. What you are looking for, I think, is for God to define the situation and to set the standard.

God Defines the Issues

Part of our paralysis in the life-and-death dilemma stems from the overwhelming nature of medical technology. The machines and the methods used by people to slice a gene or repair blood vessels seem to belong to the realm of the supernatural. There is almost a sense of awe as we enter a hospital because of what doctors can tell us about ourselves and the power over life and death they hold. The hospital's "differentness" and complexity has made it a kind of hallowed ground.

Though it seems "sacred," technology alone cannot define life and death for the Christian. We must always be suspect of technology. Don't assume that technology is equated with goodness. As with any other human endeavor, technology carries with it the expression of fallen creatures. To exercise a healthy suspicion, we must understand how God views death, health, and disability. His definitions and His heart on the issue must be a part of your vocabulary.

Death

The body is the house in which resides the spirit of a person. Without the presence of this spirit, there is no life. When Adam was created, it was not until God—the Spirit—"breathed into his nostrils the breath of life" that "man became a living being."[1] Life, for man, must include in its definition the presence of the spirit. Consider these passages from Scripture that indicate that life exists when the body and spirit are connected.

"As the body without the spirit is dead…"[2]

When Christ brought Jairus's daughter back to life, "her spirit returned and at once she stood up."[3]

And at the Crucifixion, "Jesus called out with a loud voice 'Father, into your hands I commit my spirit.' When he had said this, he breathed his last."[4]

This distinction between the body and the spirit of man is vital to remember. On the one hand, it gives the Christian facing the dilemma of death great hope to know that the destruction of the body does not mean the end of the person. "As long as we are at home in the body we are away from the Lord."[5] What a glorious promise to anyone who has had to make a decision about a loved one.

The distinction between body and spirit, on the other hand, also places great responsibility on the decision maker to know that he or she is a steward of God's breath of life.

We become decision makers in the sacred realm. As anyone in the dilemma of death will testify, that is a weighty responsibility.

Health

Many have claimed that physical health is a birthright of the Christian. "If you are walking with Christ, you will be healthy," they say. God's Word, however, tells us differently. Our bodies, because of the existence of sin since Adam, were "subjected to frustration ... in hope that the creation itself will be liberated from its bondage to decay."[6] Sickness and disease are common to all creation, including man. Indeed, unhealthiness is the norm. The fact that many of us live relatively healthy lives can be viewed as a blessing, a gift.

God will choose whom to heal and whom to keep healthy. It is not to be expected as a right or as a reward for spirituality. Paul, deemed by most of us to be "super spiritual," struggled with his own health dilemma and asked God three times to restore his health. In each case, God chose not to heal.

Disability

No one wants to be disabled or wants to have a family member with a disability, but before rejecting it as God's second best for your life, consider God's perspective.

God has a sovereign choice regarding your disability.[7]
God uses disability to bring Him glory.[8]

God uses disability to conform his church to his image.[9]

God uses disability to comfort others.[10]

God holds wonderful promises for people with disabilities.[11]

I am biased, I know, but I believe deeply that people with disabilities are God's favorite children. Jesus spent time and energy ministering to them while He was on earth. Twenty-four of the thirty-five miracles He performed were with disabled people. His ministry among disabled people served as a sign of his Messiahship.[12] And His vision for church growth was that of a house full of people with disabilities. "Go out quickly into the streets and alleys and bring in the poor, the crippled, the blind, and the lame ... and make them come in, so that my house will be full."[13]

Though the world may define disability in terms of what a person cannot do, God views people with disabilities as having a place of honor in the church.

Setting Standards

The preceding perspectives will be valuable to you as you make a decision. But equally important is to know on what standard of measure one relies when facing a dilemma. You are not shy about making a decision, perhaps, but you want to know what is important to God.

God's standards can give great comfort as well as courage to make a godly choice. In the life-and-death - dilemma, there are three standards of measure to which we must pay close attention: Life is measured by value, not quality. Good is to be chosen over rightness. And decisions are to be viewed in the context of eternity, not time and space.

Value, Not Quality

The phrase "quality of life," has recently generated widespread concern. Fifty years ago people who broke their necks as I did—died. There is no need to worry about quality of life when you're dead.

Today it's a different story. Within the last few decades, medical technology has given us high-tech helps to improve a person's so-called quality of life. And this has granted society the power to control whether a person lives or dies, all depending on the application of a few technological gizmos or newfangled drugs. A respirator enables a polio quadriplegic, like my friend Lily, to breathe. A sophisticated drug stabilizes the emotions of my neighbor Linda, who struggles with a manic-depression disorder. An indwelling catheter regulates the urinary plumbing of someone like me.

Kidney machines, pacemakers, insulin injections, and even medication, to manage either pain or depression—all of these things, to one degree or another, increase one's "quality of life."

However, by virtue of those high-tech gizmos or drug therapies, people's lives begin to be defined by whether or not they can function. Lily, thanks to a respirator, is able to sit up in a wheelchair and go about life as a "normal" person. People in pain or depression, like Linda can, with medication, hold down a job and raise a family. They can function, and thus society moves them up a few notches on its so-called quality-of-life scale, a few notches above others less able, such as my friend Bob, who is rapidly deteriorating from Lou Gehrig's disease and can only lie in bed and blink his eyes.

Some say that a society that measures people in terms of their quality of life will preserve those who have a potential to function and neglect those who don't. Oddly enough, society will ascribe to physically fit and intellectually capable people a very high quality of life, despite the fact that they are sometimes the most miserable. Yet society will ascribe a very low quality of life to poor, debilitated people, despite the fact that they are sometimes the most content.

Making decisions in the midst of a life-and-death dilemma cannot be based on the quality-of-life standard, because it is man's standard of measure and not God's. Fortunately, God has given a standard of measure that transcends the flaws inherent in the quality-of-life argument. God does not measure based on quality but rather on value. He places intrinsic value on life itself, without any evaluation as to the type of life a person might experience. If He did set such standards, none of us would be alive. As Paul said, we all "fall short of the glory of God."[14]

Just how much is a person worth? The answer might surprise you. First, consider what Jesus said in Mark 8:36–37, about the value of your life (NASB):

For what does it profit a man to gain the whole world, and forfeit his soul? For what shall a man give in exchange for his soul?

Your life is being compared here with the worth of the world. So try this mental exercise. Add up the value of all the oil reserves in the world as well as all the gold reserves. Add to that the combined value of all the usable real estate in the world, including the buildings. Add a few trinkets like platinum, silver, and diamonds to the pile. Then add just one year's gross national product for all the countries in the world. How many zeros would you see at the end of the number? Quite a number of them, wouldn't you?

Now here is the amazing part. Jesus said that you are *more* valuable than the whole world! No amount of monetary value can be applied to your life! There is nothing in this world to which the quality of your life can be compared because it is life itself that has value.

And where does this value come from?

Simply because God created you. His creative act gave life a protection of His divine favor that could not be sold. We are precious masterpieces because a master made us. And though sin marred the image, God's intrinsic value in life did not change. That means that every person born or afflicted with a marring condition still has intrinsic worth.

Gary Smalley shares an object lesson in his series on relationships. In it, he holds up an old, junky violin. The bridge is broken off, the strings are loose. It looks as though it ought to be thrown away.

But Gary holds the violin out to the audience so that they can read what is written on the inside: Stradivarius. "Do you know how much this is worth?" he asks. "This violin here is worth about $100,000!" The audience gasps at the figure, especially in light of the violin's appearance.

The violin is worth that much, not because of its condition but because of its maker. The damage made no difference. It was the name on the inside that counted.

You and I, likewise, have the signature of God on each of us. That name makes us priceless, and no economic or functional or emotional standard can be placed on it, even when we are damaged beyond what people would say is a person.

Good, Not Right

A second standard of measure we must keep in mind is based on one of God's attributes: goodness. God is good and requires that His created beings exercise goodness. This is basic Sunday school theology, but I emphasize this because we have substituted the standard of rightness. Hospitals and nursing homes have policies. States have laws. Even our culture has customs that dictate behavior. These "codes" carry with them the air of authority.

I am not advocating anarchy, but be careful not to assume that what is "right" according to society and its institutions is necessarily "good." "Right" speaks of being correct. "Good" speaks of being righteous. And it is righteousness we are to seek.

The Pharisees were good at the right and wrong game. They had distilled God's good law down to over six hundred rights and wrongs. And oh, were they right! Make no mistake, they practiced what they preached!

Look at Jesus' response to the rightness of the Pharisees.

> Going on from that place, he went into their synagogue, and a man with a shriveled hand was there. Looking for a reason to accuse Jesus, they asked him, "Is it lawful to heal on the Sabbath?"
> He said to them, "If any of you has a sheep and it falls into a pit on the Sabbath, will you not take hold of it and lift it out? How much more valuable is a man than a sheep! *Therefore, it is lawful to do good on the Sabbath.*" [15]

How does this difference play out in the life-and-death dilemma? Evaluate each policy or law, and if you discern that it violates God's standard of good as revealed in the Bible, seek recourse to allow yourself to exercise good.

Eternal, Not Temporal

> "All men are like grass, and all their glory is like the flowers of the field. The grass withers and the flowers fall, because the breath of the Lord blows on them. Surely the people are grass." [16]

In case you haven't noticed, all people die. They don't live forever. We are indeed like grass, destined for "mulchhood" since the day we were born. Our finiteness can cause us to wonder if we have any link with the vast expanse of time. Will the decision you make in the life-and-death dilemma, for example, have any impact one hundred years from now? A million years from now? In heaven?

Notice God's answer to man's finiteness immediately following the above verse. "The grass withers and the flowers fall, but the word of our God stands forever."[17] Such a standard is vital for making a decision, because if God's word stands forever, then your decision made in light of that word will also stand forever. Any choice we make in accordance with the will of God carries with it a promise of significance and eternal consequence. His word will not return void. We are promised a reward for the work we do upon the foundation of Christ.

In concrete terms, consider the impact of the following decision. Suppose that you authorize the removal of life supports from someone you know is not a Christian. Such a decision will have eternal consequences for that individual. Or consider the impact on your children should you file for divorce from your disabled spouse. Can you risk the eternal as well as lifelong consequences of such an action?

An eternal perspective not only helps you make a better decision, it can also help you bear up under the crisis. Isaiah's words are actually comforting. We will not long have to endure the scourges of life because we are like grass. We won't have to endure suffering forever. I know, the crisis you are experiencing has gone on a long time and seems endless. But believe me, it will be over someday. And to hasten it with an ill-advised decision will be a source of regret for you. Weigh the time you will endure in your crisis against the weight of eternity, and you will gain new courage and a better understanding of God's heart on the matter.

Off the Beach

We've spent some time on the beach, examining God's view of the battle scene. "But so what?" you ask. "What difference does it make? How will I know that using God's standards and definitions will have any impact or matter to God? Why not just choose to end it all and get it over with?"

Such questions are to be expected in light of what people in society are saying about their choices and having understood God's perspective and standard of measure. It's time now to see just how important your decision is and to equip you with a defense for those who will tell you that it's okay to let go.

Discussion Guide

God Defines

1. Joni and others assert that death from a Christian perspective occurs when the spirit leaves the body. Discuss how you might determine when that happens? Use as many medical and scriptural criteria as you can find.

2. Did you have difficulty arriving at a precise method of discerning the time of death? You probably had a difficult time coming to a conclusion. If it is difficult to determine, how should one proceed when making a decision regarding death?

3. Do you agree with Joni's assertion that God allows illness and disability? What do Job and passages like John 9:1–5 say about the subject?

4. If God does allow such things to happen, what impact could such knowledge have on people facing a crisis?

Making Decisions

Michael is a 23-year-old who was recently in an automobile accident. His injuries to the head were quite extensive, and doctors believe he is in a "locked-in" position. He seems to be aware of things happening in the room but is unresponsive most of the time. During his

stay at the hospital, he experienced respiratory failure.
His doctors put him on a ventilator. His parents want it
turned off.

1. List the key facts in the case above that are relevant to the decision and then make a decision.

2. Given these facts, what would you advise if you were the family's pastor?

3. After discussing the case with others in the group, what values did you hear being expressed? In other words, what standards did people hold as most important?

    What definitions did they use in presenting their reasons?

4. In analyzing Michael's case, what motives do you think the parents had in not wanting the respirator on? What were the doctor's motives? Which motives do you think should take precedence, if any?

PART TWO

Does It Matter?

Have you ever had to put together a toy or a piece of furniture following a set of printed instructions? You carefully lay out all the parts to your left, keeping the instructions to your right, and then very carefully start at Step 1. Things go fairly well until about midway through when the maze of instructions and the object you are creating in front of you blurs into a potential disaster. You read the line that says "Be sure to lock widget z to crankle c, but before doing so, leave about ¼ inch of space . . ."

You realize you have to make a decision, but the confusion and the frustration level is high. You look at widget z and crankle c, but they look nothing like the picture in the instructions. And upon further study, you observe that these parts seem superfluous. "It doesn't look like they matter much," you say. You wing the rest of the project, glancing now and then at the pictures and at your project. But when the project is finally built, you realize it won't work or stand up straight.

Why not?

Because widget z and crankle c *did* matter. They made a difference after all.

You might be at a similar point in your dilemma. You have been faithful up to this point in hearing God's promises and recognizing the difference between the world's reasons for giving up and God's reasons for holding fast. But it still seems too theoretical—as if all of this so far has been meant for the general rule, the ideal. You realize that there are multitudes of people making all kinds of choices in anonymity, and you don't see either the good or ill effects of the choices. You wonder about the significance or importance of the choices you must make. Does it really matter what I choose to do? What difference does it make to the person I love? To me?

Those are honest and valid questions. You need to know, and in a sense, have earned the right to know, the bottom line of your decision. Because if it didn't matter— if God's wisdom were just an option or icing on the cake— then why make choices that are difficult or that require sacrifice?

When a decision is difficult, we often want to avoid it or walk away. And the first thing we excuse ourself with is, "It doesn't matter." This is especially true in the realm of decisions with which God is intimately involved. Matters such as life, morality, and relationships often get shrug-shoulder treatment.

It does matter. Your decision to withhold treatment, or forego surgery, or walk out on a relationship does have an impact. There is profound significance in what you decide. And you might be surprised at the scope of that significance.

This section tells you why it matters and to whom it matters. For the sake of simplicity, the discussion focuses on just one kind of dilemma, namely death. The arguments, however, apply to other dilemmas of health and disability as well.

4

YOUR DECISION
MATTERS TO OTHERS

For the moment, forget everything you've ever read in either a right-to-die or a right-to-life brochure. Put aside the court rulings. Push out of your mind the tug-at-your-heart stories you've read in the newspapers.

Now, with no one reading your thoughts, may I ask: Do you know when it is right to die? For you? For your family? Please, I realize this may not be a theoretical question for you. You may be one who could write a real-life tug-at-your-heart story. And you may have already made up your mind about how and when you want to die. Whatever your response, I want you to know that your decision matters.

It matters more than you realize.

Let me explain. Since I served on a council that drafted major civil rights legislation, my husband Ken, a high-school government teacher, asked me to speak to his classes on the subject of legalizing euthanasia. California is the testing ground for various right-to-die initiatives, and Ken wanted me to talk to his students about the implications of a right-to-die law. The classroom was crowded, with kids standing along the back wall and leaning against the side chalkboards.

I was surprised by how interested they were as I divulged my despair of earlier days. I admitted my relief that no right-to-die law existed when I was in the hospital and hooked up to machines. I then underscored how critical it is for every student to become informed and involved in shaping society's response to the problem. Then I added, "What role do you think society should play in helping people decide when it is right to die?"

A few hands went up. I could tell by their answers that they felt that society should take action to help hurting and dying people, some students insisting on life no matter how burdensome the treatment, and a few wanting to help by hurrying along the death process.

One student shared how his mother was getting demoralized by the burden of taking care of his mentally handicapped sister. He felt society should, in his words, "do something."

"Like what?" I playfully challenged.

"Like . . . I'm not sure, but society ought to get more involved in the lives of people like my mother."

I glanced at Ken. He nodded as if to give the go-ahead to take a free rein with this young man. "May I ask what you have done to get more involved?"

The student smiled and shrugged.

"How have you helped alleviate the burden? Have you taken your sister on an outing lately? Maybe to the beach?" I teased. "Have you offered to do some shopping for your mother? Maybe your mom wouldn't be so demoralized, wouldn't feel so stressed or burdened if you rolled up your sleeves a little higher to help."

A couple of his friends by the chalkboard laughed and threw wads of paper at him. "Okay, okay, I see your point," he chuckled.

I smiled. "My point is this: Society is not a bunch of people way out there who sit around big tables and think up political trends or cultural drifts. Society is you. Your actions, your decisions matter. What you do or don't do has a rippling effect on everyone around you. And even on a smaller scale, your participation can make a huge difference in what your family decides to do with your sister."

The classroom fell silent, and I knew the lesson was being driven home. I paused, scanned the face of each student, and closed, saying, "You, my friends, are society."

Your Point of View Matters

And that's how much your view matters. You may be the one who fiercely advocates pulling the plug, or the one who fights to keep a heart pumping until the bitter end. Whichever, you must, in the words of John Donne, know this:

> No man is an island entire of itself; every man is a piece of the continent, a part of the main . . . any man's death diminishes me, because I am involved in mankind; and therefore never send to know for whom the bell tolls; it tolls for thee.[1]

We are such private people. We would like to be able to make a life-and-death decision in a vacuum or even at an arm's-length distance from others, but we can't. Your point of view and how you act on it, let's say as you lie in bed with a terminal illness, not only matters to you and your family, it matters to a wide network of friends and associates. In other words, society. The cultural drift is channeled by your decision to either pull the plug or hold on to life.

In fact, will you permit me to get personal? If you can, dismiss your real-life circumstances for a moment. Let's pretend you *are* in bed with a terminal illness, and doctors say you could live for another six months. Your pain *can* be effectively managed. And you *do* have an opportunity to make a choice about prolonging medical treatment. Laws *will* permit you to decline that treatment, and your family says it's up to you. I know it's hard to pretend such an antiseptic situation, devoid of real grief and actual anguish, because distress would play a key role. But given this sterile scenario, what would you do? What would you say?

Are you one who might say, "It's none of your business. I'll control how and when I die, and what's more, I don't care about any poem by John Donne, and I feel no responsibility to society. I'm only responsible to myself and those I love."

I hear what you're saying. But when people maintain that their death is their own business and that of "those I love," they do not consider the significance of their decision on the wider circle of life. A decision to cut life short, even if only a few months, does not stop with "those I love" but affects a whole network of relationships: friends, former colleagues, teachers, distant family members, casual acquaintances, and even nurses and doctors who occasionally stop by your bedside.

Just what effect might your decision have? Your gutsy choice to face suffering head-on forces others around you to sit up and take notice. It's called strengthening the character of a helping society. When people observe perseverance, endurance, and courage, their moral fiber is reinforced. Conversely, your choice to bow out of life can and does weaken the moral resolve of that same society.

Years after my hospitalization, my mother is still receiving letters from nurses, cafeteria workers, and a family whose brain-damaged daughter was hooked up to machines two beds down from me in the intensive care unit. My parents made gutsy choices that involved facing suffering head-on. And the decisions they made regarding my care have had a lasting impact on these people. And who knows what they one day will decide if faced with life-and-death decisions?

If you believe your decision is private and independent, your choice to speed up the dying process is like playing a delicate game of Pick Up Sticks. You carefully lift a stick, hoping not to disturb the intricate web. But just when you think you've succeeded, your independent action ends up jiggling the fragile balance.

And as it says in the Bible, "None of us lives to himself alone and none of us dies to himself alone."[2]

You Have Your Rights . . . Sort of

"But I have a right to decide what's best for me. I'm entitled to exercise my independence. It's fundamental to what this country is all about. Even the courts recognize my autonomy as a patient."

True, as a mentally competent person, the judge would probably bang the gavel in your favor. As you said, you have rights, and you may end up literally dying for them.

But like all other liberties, your choice is not absolute—no ifs, ands, or buts. Your self-determination to die has strings attached if it adversely affects the rights of others. That's why more than half the states in our country have laws against aiding a person in suicide. Think it through: If everybody ended his or her life as a solution to problems, the very fabric of our society would ultimately unravel, and with it all the other individual rights you enjoy.

Yes, you have a glistening right of privacy, as long as it does not overshadow the rights of others. For this reason, legalized euthanasia could seriously infringe on the rights of many physicians. You might want to exercise a right to die, but you cannot ask a physician, whose duty is to heal, to comply with your wishes, or to even make a referral. No person, in the name of self-determination, can oblige a doctor to inject him with orphenadrine when it goes against the physician's oath to heal.

But wait; it sounds a little like we're trading baseball cards here.

Like, "My rights are more valuable than yours!"

"Oh, yeah? Well, my one right is worth more than your three combined!"

Our rights are not things that can be exchanged, bargained over, or transferred like property. Essentially, rights are *moral claims* to be recognized by law, not things to be traded.[3] And moral claims have to take into account responsibility, limits on freedom, and ethical standards that reflect the good of the entire community.

When we clamor about the sanctity of our individual rights, we may be reinforcing an all-too-human failing—the tendency to place ourselves at the center of the moral universe. We label our desires "rights" as if to give those willful determinations a showy kind of dignity. If taken to the extreme, radical clamor over individual rights can lead to one indignation after another about the inherent limitations of society, and we will never be satisfied.

As I shared in Ken's government class, "You, my friends, are society." So, welcome to the club of community, and even though you may try to drown out other styles of discourse with your shout over personal rights, the community around you may have a thing or two to say, and they may say it a lot louder. After all, community can only progress when its individuals exercise higher moral choices, and community is sacrificed when individuals choose with only themselves in mind.

God's Laws Make for a Better Society and Vice Versa

Are you with me? For the sake of argument, remember our sterile scenario: You're still in that bed with a terminal illness and a choice to make. Yes, I realize it's hard to think about such things as "moral claims" and "the good of society" when you're approaching death's door, but bear with me. Hold on to the guardrail of that hospital bed, and let's broaden the scenario a bit.

Picture yourself biding time and glancing occasionally at the television bolted to the ceiling at the foot of your bed. The evening news is on, and the commentator launches into the story at the top of the hour.

"Within days," he announces, "voters will have an opportunity to pass a state initiative that would legally permit a terminally ill patient to request a lethal injection from his doctor."

The news commentator drones on, but your mind is already racing. *This is the answer,* you think, *the answer for thousands of terminally ill people who would never buy John Donne's rhetoric or a lot of sympathetic mush about "the good of society."* Make legal the right to die, and everything is taken care of: No more families going bankrupt because of outrageous hospital bills, not to mention the burden to Medicare or insurance companies. And no more parents biting their nails over what to do with their daughter in a long-drawn-out coma. Simply make legal the right to die, and if legislators don't have the guts to do it, then get it on the state ballot, and let public sentiment pass the law.

Take the scenario even further. You pick up the phone on your bedside stand, dial a family member, and tell him to grab your absentee ballot from the pile of mail on the kitchen table—before you arrive at death's door, you want to leave an epitaph and vote yes on this thing!

It sounds good and, like one of my husband's students, I admire your desire to get involved. But wait a minute. Let's say that the bulk of voters share your sentiments. They flock to the polls and pass the initiative into law. In fact, "as recently as the fall elections of 1994, one state in the U.S. passed an initiative that now makes it legal for physicians in that state to prescribe a lethal dose of drugs at the request of a terminally ill person who has less than six months to live. There are other stipulations and limitations on this new law, but suffice it to say, it's not merely a crack in the door. The door has now been kicked open, and the stage is set for expanded and more liberal changes in the law; in fact, a lot of other doors in states around the country may soon be opening to legalized euthanasia."

What Now?

Just picture the future brave new world that is created. ***Physicians are cast in the role of killer, not healer.*** For 2400 years terminally ill, dying, and debilitated persons have had the assurance that doctors operate under an oath to heal them, not kill them. Under legalized euthanasia, the Hippocratic Oath is being turned upside down, and patient trust in doctors is seriously eroding. In fact, a fringe element in the medical community is beginning to act rashly, ending the lives of "difficult" patients rather than taking the time and effort to offer truly compassionate care.

Standard medical care is being seriously undermined. Elderly and severely disabled patients are not receiving the same quality of care as everyone else. Legalized euthanasia is resulting in less care for the dying, rather than better care as the medical community shifts its focus to cure and rehabilitate. It's a matter of economics: Euthanasia is extraordinarily cheap when compared with the costs of humane chronic and terminal care.

Legalized euthanasia establishes a fundamental right to die. The U.S. Constitution affirms that fundamental rights cannot be limited to any one group, such as the terminally ill. The door is now open to court challenges allowing suicide-on-demand for everyone: clinically depressed persons, children with cystic fibrosis, nursing home residents, people with AIDS, and those with large medical bills. Because all now enjoy an "equal protection of being killed," no one is denied aid in dying, especially those who cannot request it for themselves, such as people in comas or in persistent vegetative states.[4]

Legalized euthanasia broadens the application of the right to die. Vulnerable people, such as the poor, the senile, and those uninsured, are being pressured into euthanizing themselves in order to relieve the economic burden they place on society. Patients who are misdiagnosed are falling through the cracks of the new law. Many families are discovering that, without their knowledge, their loved ones are being killed.

The character of a helping society is beginning to disintegrate. Euthanasia is now seen as a cure-all to societal problems such as rising public-health-care costs and limited facility space for elderly and debilitated people. It's easier to kill than cure, or even care. Society is now assigning no positive value to suffering and is becoming more oriented toward a culture of comfort. Discrimination against elderly and disabled people is beginning to run rampant—terms such as "useless victim" and "unfortunates to be pitied" reveal a growing cynicism and bigotry. Before euthanasia became legalized, hospice organizations and handicap associations had difficulty securing funding and volunteer support. Now, with the new law, these agencies are having more trouble than ever.

Legalized Euthanasia: A Good Law for a Better Society?

Does that brave-new-world scenario sound farfetched?

Believe me, it's closer to home than you think. Right now in Europe there is a country where all this is beginning to happen. Although euthanasia is not legalized in Holland, the courts are turning a blind eye to thousands of terminally ill patients who are being euthanized by physicians. Some reports indicate that half the doctors in Holland who offer "aid in dying" have killed conscious patients without bothering to get consent.[5]

Perhaps you think that could never happen here in the good ol' U.S. of A.: "We would never let that occur in our country. Laws are meant to protect people, and legalizing euthanasia would just apply to those who want to die."

Not necessarily. The hotly emotional debate surrounding euthanasia underscores just how dynamic an issue it is. And dynamic issues in society never remain static, they are constantly evolving, and laws are forever being revised to accommodate the changes. Advocates will say, "Well, right-to-die legislation was put on the books to *respond* to the terminally ill, but now we must *extend* the same legal rights to the comatose. And how about *amending* the law to include the severely mentally retarded? And AIDS is a pandemic, so let's campaign to *modify* the law to include anyone who has the HIV virus."

I'm not being an alarmist. Even quadriplegics like me are at risk! "What can those of us who sympathize with a justified suicide by a handicapped person do to help?" asks Derek Humphry of The Hemlock Society. His answer gives me the jitters: "When we have statutes on the books permitting lawful physician aid-in-dying for the terminally ill, I believe that, along with this reform, there will come a more tolerant attitude toward other exceptional cases."[6]

No, I'm not a doomsday prophet when I say that legalizing the right to die is like taking a crowbar to Pandora's box. Pry that lever under the lid with a single law and you've opened the whole box, exposing the entire population to "equal protection for being killed." Once legalized, the logical end of euthanasia is sheer terror. So why even get behind it in the first place?

There must be a better way. There has to be a different answer. No, I haven't forgotten the scenario that you're lying in bed with a terminal illness and facing perhaps a difficult and uncomfortable death in six months.

And yes, I realize that we have yet to answer tough, distressing questions about tubes, machines, and life-support systems. But I will not abandon you after hospital visiting hours are over. I have more to say. I promise.

Dear Joni,

My name is Carol Walters. I was born with cerebral palsy—I walk with a limp and my hands I can use, but I have poor control.

I was thinking how I don't think a handicapped person should take his or her life anymore than anyone else. I feel we are here to live our lives to contribute to our place where we live. Everyone has something to offer.

I have a part-time job at city hall in my town. At work I am known as Smiley. I clean up the community building and I sweep walks. I feel God has put me at that job for a reason. I think that reason is to help people realize that I can live a full and happy life the way I am.

I do have moments feeling sorry for myself and there are times I wish God would make me normal. I talk to my mom and she helps me see that I have many blessings.

Love,
Carol Walters

Discussion Guide

No Man Is an Island

Helen is a 43-year-old woman with cancer. Though her cancer had been relatively mild for some time, her condition has rapidly worsened. She has had several bouts of depression. Her three kids have handled the situation surprisingly well, but it is beginning to wear on them and on her husband. She has gone through several kinds of treatments. The latest report from the doctor indicated she is a candidate for a bone-marrow transplant. Helen does not want to have the transplant done.

1. Who would be affected by Helen's decision referred to in the scenario? Any others that would be affected by her decision who are not referred to in the story?

2. If Helen did not have the transplant, what impact would it have on the family? How do you think each would respond?

3. Helen is a devoted mother. It's hard to think she wouldn't consider the impact on her family. Assuming she has thought about the impact, what conclusions do you think she came to that led her to believe that trying the transplant was not worth it? Here are some examples:

   "My family needs to get on with their life. This is depressing them, and my marriage could fall apart."

"We can't afford the surgery. College bills are coming in just a few years."

"I'll take my chances without the transplant."

Given Helen's reasons, do you still agree with her?

5

Your Decision Matters to You

We are now at the part where I wish there were no pages between us. I'd give anything if I could wheel up to your bedside, past the bleeping machines and dripping tubes, to talk face-to-face. Or be with you at your kitchen table to hear your heartache over your senile mother in a nursing home. Or just sit and listen as you lift the black cloak of depression long enough to speak.

If we were together, I'd want to talk about facing suffering: the kind that spins out of control, rips into your sanity, and tears apart your body—the kind of suffering that helpful information is powerless against.

If we were together, I'd want to peel back our defenses and confess how we both would really rather leapfrog the whole process of pain. How we'd like to detour the distress and shortcut the suffering. Many say that life is something to be discarded when it does not work properly or seem to have value, when it is a constant struggle to hold on to it. How much easier to bypass it all.

Leapfrogging the Process of Pain

No thinking person chooses suffering. But we can choose our attitude in the midst of suffering.

That was a lesson driven home to me when years ago, in college, I read *Man's Search for Meaning*, a classic study of how people preserve their spiritual freedom and heroic responses in the face of horrible suffering. The author, Viktor Frankl, was a psychiatrist who was sent to a concentration camp in World War II in which he found himself stripped to naked existence, cold, starved, beaten, and expecting extermination with each passing day. He lost his friends and family to the gas ovens. He lost every valued possession. How could he find life worth preserving?

The book hit home to me as a college student, even though campus life was far from the terrors of Auschwitz. Viktor Frankl's work meant much more to me during the darkest, loneliest days of my two-year confinement in the hospital. There, lying face down, strapped on a Stryker frame, I turned each page of *Man's Search for Meaning* with a mouthstick clutched between my teeth. My tears would drop and splatter on pages where this camp survivor wrote:

> We who lived in concentration camps can remember the men who walked through the huts, comforting others, giving away their last piece of bread. They may have been few in number, but they offer sufficient proof that everything can be taken from a man but one thing: the last of the human freedoms—to choose one's attitude in any given set of circumstances.
>
> And there were always choices to make. Every day, every hour, offered the opportunity to make a decision, a decision to those powers which threatened to rob you of your very self, your inner freedom;

which determined whether or not you would become the plaything of circumstance.

This man was worlds apart from my vocational-rehab counselor. He had been there, and so his words commanded my attention. I remember pausing to give my mouth a break from page turning, murmuring over and over, "I am *not* held hostage by my handicap. . . . I am *not* held hostage by my handicap." Mine was not so much a spiritual exercise but a mental effort, a first-step attempt at breaking free of the circumstances that had dug their claws of control into me. I would read on:

> Even though conditions such as lack of sleep, insufficient food and various mental stresses may suggest that the inmates were bound to react in certain ways, in the final analysis it becomes clear that the sort of person the prisoner became was the result of an *inner decision*, not the result of camp influences alone . . . When we are no longer able to change a situation— just think of an incurable disease such as inoperable cancer—we are challenged to change ourselves. [1]

I was challenged to change myself. But how? I felt a little sheepish that my inner decision could barely move me to smile in my wheelchair, let alone face with courage things like starvation, beatings, and gas ovens.

When I finished Viktor Frankl's book, I realized it was an answer to one basic question, a question that, in fact, the psychiatrist, after he was released and returned to his practice, often asked his troubled patients: "Why do you not commit suicide?"

In other words, "Why do you not leapfrog suffering?"

From their answers it was then the goal of the psychiatrist to weave these slender threads of a broken life into a pattern of meaning. Each person, he insisted, could find valuable meaning in suffering.

I mused over the meaning to my suffering while lying right-side-up on my Stryker frame rather than upside down—it was easier to think hopeful thoughts than facing fresh air than the floor! As I counted the tiles on the ceiling, I counted the few, slender, bright-shining threads of my broken life.

I'm alive.

I can at least still feel in my neck and tops of my shoulders.

I can see the moon through my hospital window.

I'm learning that patience and endurance means more on a Stryker frame than running twenty-five laps around a hockey field.

My friends are still coming to see me, and the doughnuts they bring taste good. It's nice to have the nurse read me Robert Frost's poetry during her lunch break. I like listening to the Beatles.

And, like holding on to a thin kite string, I have hope that it might get better. I see it in the eyes and smiles of my family, my friends, and a few of the nurses. Oh, and one more positive thing—they might find a cure for spinal-cord injury!

Small as they were, these slender threads tied me to life, even if I hadn't yet decided if it was worth living. The threads were fragile, but they held me through the day and kept me connected to people. The meaning behind it all, however, was still unclear, but I knew this much: It had something to do with God.

Someone said that if you believe that the individual is supreme, then your responsibility is only to yourself since there is no God who gives us life or who awaits us in death. But if you believe that life derives from a loving Creator, then leapfrogging the suffering process must be considered within a larger context.[2]

It was a fact that my background oriented me toward God. And my assessment about life and death was becoming a matter of conscience rather than a knee-jerk reaction to the problems at hand. Weeks passed. My thoughts deepened. And the longer I hung in there through the process of suffering, the stronger the weave in the fabric of meaning. I was convinced that God was mysteriously behind the pattern, so I took a closer look at new threads.

My friendships are deepening and becoming more honest.

What's important in life is people.

I'm learning the value of a smile.

God is real. I can feel Him when I am alone at night.

There are others who are hurting a lot more than I am, and I'm beginning to care, honestly care, about them.

What were once thin, slender threads were now becoming cords. And the fabric of meaning behind my suffering was beginning to take shape. Life, I was discovering, was worth living.

Talking About the "G" Word

I know I've brought up a delicate subject for some. Even medical ethicists all but banish God from their discussions and writings. And those who help set moral and medical standards in hospitals tend to confine the subject of God to the hospital chapel. But let's be honest—prayer and God are as commonplace in hospitals as bedpans and bottles of pills.

So let's have a quick rehab lesson here. Traditional rehabilitation philosophy will pull out all the stops to address a patient's physical, psychological, emotional, and vocational needs, while spiritual needs are at best ignored. But more professionals are beginning to see that the rehabilitation of a person's spirit is key in affecting all those other areas. A healthy and whole spirit affects everything, from a patient's attitude and motivation to his everyday relationships. Why? Because how a person relates to God has a profound influence on what he thinks about himself, his goals, and his friends and family. It has something to do with responding to "higher authority" and a source of "absolute value."

A disabled person who connects with God usually demonstrates personal freedom, responsibility to the community, true achievement, and meaningful relationships with people. And what if a person ignores God and sets himself up at the center of his own moral universe? Well, those who remain masters of their own lives to the exclusion of God and others will inevitably negate themselves. As the Vatican papers have stated, "Man, who is alienated from the Source of Life, his Creator, expresses his dominion over his own life by destroying it."

Of course, theologians would jump in here and have much more to say, but for now it's safe to underscore that relating with God can bring about the foundational stability of peace in a patient's life. Peace with the One in charge . . . peace with circumstances . . . and peace with oneself.

Is Weaving the Threads Worth the Effort?

So much for me. And so much for Viktor Frankl.

But a death camp survivor and a quadriplegic simply can't paste our experiences on others who want to leapfrog their suffering. What would Viktor Frankl say to someone like Larry McAfee, a civil engineer paralyzed from the neck down by a 1985 motorcycle accident and sustained on a ventilator?

And what could I say to Larry McAfee? Unable to move out of a nursing home and unable to breathe on his own, Larry asked the courts to allow him to pull the plug on his ventilator so that he could die. The court petition simply stated that Larry "has no control over his person and receives no enjoyment out of life."[3] I wasted no time before writing to Larry.

Dear Larry,

Like you, I've experienced being reduced to just existing—the basics of breathing, eating, and sleeping. Lying there, I felt as though my experience represented every human (it's just that the rest of the human race didn't realize they were merely breathing and sleeping—they were too busy being on their feet with a lot of distractions). After much thinking I realized that there *had* to be more to life for everybody than just mere existence. And if not, then why not everybody "pull the plug" no matter if they were disabled or not!

In a way, I felt as though Viktor Frankl were looking over my shoulder from his bunkbed in that concentration camp. He, too, would agree that there had to be more to life than just existing, going through the motions, getting born, then growing old, and then dying.[4] But I wanted to take it a step further from the advice of the psychiatrist; I wanted to talk to Larry about how I connected with God.

At that point, I came to the conclusion that there has to be a personal God who cares for me and everybody else if, indeed, life is to make sense. There must be a God . . . and if not, then the whole human race should put a gun to its collective head if it wants to. But humans are unique, too significant to just put ourselves out of our misery if we can't handle suffering. No, there must be a God who cares. There *must* be.

As I wrote, I wished there were no pages between Larry and me. I would have given anything to wheel into his room and angle my chair close to his bed so he could see me through the tubes and machines. If we were together, I'd confess how I, too, at one time wanted to leapfrog the process of pain.

And I would tell Larry that God knew exactly how we both felt. God isn't holed up in an ivory tower in the corner of the universe. He suffered, too. Even Jesus was tempted to give in. He even sought, if possible, to avoid the suffering of the cross, pleading, "Father, if You are willing, take this cup from me." In the Garden of Gethsemane as the shadow of his death approached, he felt alone and distressed, with no one around who could understand. So He turned to His Father, the only one He could talk to, ". . . And being in anguish, he prayed more earnestly."[5]

I would also tell Larry that Jesus' decision to face the Cross squarely, secured a deeper meaning for the suffering of us all. More meaning than we could possibly imagine.

As I dropped my letter to Larry into the mailbox, I hoped he would find his own few bright-shining threads of meaning. But the next day I saw a headline in the newspaper, "Judge rules quadriplegic can end life at will." My shoulders slumped when I also read, "'The ventilator to which he is attached is not prolonging his life; it is prolonging his death,' said the judge." A petition included an affidavit stating "I understand turning off the ventilator will result in my death," signed by a shaky "X" made with a pencil held in McAfee's mouth.[6]

That made me, an activist and advocate, steaming mad! If that judge had been approached by a poor minority woman who could no longer endure racism, sexism, and poverty, and she wanted aid to end her life painlessly, the woman would have been refused flat-out. In fact, she would be offered support in seeking better housing and a job. But when a disabled person like Larry McAfee declares the same intention, people assume that he is acting rationally.

Back to Larry's story. What happened next was somewhat confusing. For some reason he decided not to have himself removed from the respirator. Next, Larry was transferred from the nursing home to another facility. His story dropped out of the papers, and I was unable to hunt up his new address. I had no idea where Larry was or what he was thinking, but I kept pulling for him from a distance, hoping that he would find those threads of meaning for his life.

Finally, after several years, I tracked him down. I was itching to find out why he decided to live, so I called him up. We chatted for a few moments, talking about quadriplegia and pressure sores, and then I got a little more serious. "Larry," I asked, "why did you decide not to follow through on assisted suicide? What was your reason to keep on living?"

He managed to speak in between huffs and puffs of his respirator. "Because I'm not forced to live in an institution or hospital anymore. I'm living in a little independent-living house with two other guys in wheelchairs. It's a lot more enjoyable with a lot less pressure, less rigid. You can set your own schedule. As long as I'm not forced to live under the conditions of the state, then I consider life worth living."

My eyes lit up. I inhaled deeply and then let it out slowly. He was right. Too many debilitated people feel trapped, even warehoused in institutions. Saving people's lives and rehabilitating them is pointless if they are denied the means to control their lives. I prodded him a bit more. "So it's a chance to forge friendships, pursue hobbies?"

"Yeah, just to feel more human."

"What was it like in the institution?"

Larry paused a moment. "I just existed from day to day. But here I'm able to meet people on an equal basis."

This man sounded as though he had found his bright-shining threads. Slender, just a few, but threads strong enough to weave meaning into his life. As I listened, I kept whispering thanks under my breath. As John Donne had written, Larry's death would have diminished me, especially me, another quadriplegic!

I dared one more question. "Any advice you can give to people who, like you and me, can't use their hands or legs, maybe in wheelchairs?"

The line was quiet, and I could tell he was thinking. "I'll be honest. If a person, after years of trying, feels like he can't go on, then I feel it's within his right to . . . well, you know."

My spirits sagged a little. But I was thankful that he, at least, felt like he *could* go on. And I took comfort from the fact that his decision to live had most assuredly inspired others to do the same. Just then Larry added, "But I'd tell them, 'Don't rush into any hasty decisions but give things a lot of thought and time. Don't try to conform to society. Give it time. Seek some guidance, not only from God but friends and family.'"

Friends.

Family.

God.

These were the bright-shining threads in his life. Warm, caring, available people who accepted him, brought him out of social isolation, listened to his anger, helped him discover truth about himself, and encouraged him to interpret his future as a friend.[7]

How did they do it? They were people who circumvented the crippling health-care system that had sentenced him to an institution and denied him the self-determination to live independently. They were the people who put together the concept of the little independent-living center, who recognized Larry's freedom to set his own schedule and live as he wished. They were people who became his friends at the center, and from what he said at the close of our phone conversation, perhaps even helped him find God.[8]

Larry learned what every hurting person who chooses life discovers: *Answers most often come in the form of people rather than sentences.*

Helpful Information and . . .

People. I don't think Larry would have made it without them. His was a burden that needed bearing. His misery needed mercy. He didn't need an argument, a rational discussion, or placement in a suicide-prevention program. What he needed was a few people ready to give practical love, the kind of love that has its sleeves rolled up. And Larry's friends weren't the type to point him to a cross-stitched proverb set behind glass in a pretty frame. They helped him live information, love it, fight it, breathe it, and make it his own.

Men and women said to Larry, "Choose life."

Friends said to me, "Believe in God."

Even Viktor Frankl said to thousands in despair, "Suffering can have meaning."

And thankfully, these people did not wad up truths into platitudes to be tossed at us who hurt, while they stood at a respectable arm's-length distance. "Believe in God" glowed with the warm heartbeat of love that was as real as flesh and blood. "Choose life" were words spoken straight ahead with a smile that involved, that invited. "Suffering can have meaning" was the covering that gently enfolded.

Helpful information is not enough. No one comes out of despair alive without a caring friend on the other side. For . . .

> Two are better than one, because they have a good return for their work: If one falls down, his friend can help him up. But pity the man who falls and has no one to help him up!
>
> Ecclesiastes 4:9–10

You cannot, you must not suffer alone. It matters to the point of life and death.

Discussion Guide

It's About You

You've spent time deciding on other people's scenarios. Now it's time to write your own. About you! Choose a dilemma—death, health, or disability—and make up a scenario with some pertinent details.

Now answer the following questions and share them with the group.

1. What impact will the medical crisis you've described have on you? Be honest. You know how you've responded to crises in the past. Use that experience to picture what would happen to you:

   Emotionally

   In your relationship with other people

   In your relationship with God

2. What good do you think could come out of your situation?

3. How might you grow in your relationship with God?

4. What might you pray in the midst of your dilemma?

6

YOUR DECISION MATTERS
TO THE ENEMY

I'll never forget the first day of my marriage to Ken. What a carefree, delightful morning!

As our jet lifted off from Los Angeles to fly us to our honeymoon in Hawaii, we cuddled and kissed. The flight attendants giggled and presented us with a cake and a couple of leis. After they served refreshments, we settled back and put on the earphones to watch the in-flight movie. To my surprise, it was *Whose Life Is It Anyway!*— the film about a quadriplegic who tried to get everyone, from his friends to his doctor to his lawyer, to permit him the right to die.

Ken and I pulled off our earphones. This was not the time to think about the depression of quadriplegia or the desire it often brings to cut one's life short.

As the opening credits appeared on the screen, the flight attendant knelt by my seat and whispered, "Oh, Mrs. Tada, I'm very sorry about the movie selection today. Shall we change your seat?"

I smiled and shook my head to the contrary. I knew I had hope and a future, although I had a difficult time the rest of the flight convincing the attendants that I was not bothered by the visual images on the screen. Yet even as Ken and I snuggled and talked of our future, I kept sneaking peeks at the film.

Without the soundtrack, strange and twisted thoughts began to whisper and wheedle into my brain. *Does Ken really know what he's gotten himself into? What if we can't handle it? Divorce and suicide happen to couples like us all the time. What if . . .*

Hold it! This was the happiest day of my life, and I refused to entertain such deplorable thoughts! I shook my head, jerked my attention away from the movie, and riveted it totally on Ken. I wasn't about to allow subtle ideas, like flying birds, to build a nest in my head.

It's called resisting temptation.

A provoking thought. A strong inclination. An inducement. An enticement to give in and give up. A crazy idea that settles in and begins to sound pleasing and plausible.

Thoughts leading to death begin that way.

I've had enough experience with temptation to know that such provocations aren't furtive ideas that dart out of nowhere, disjointed, and having no connection. There exists an intelligence behind those ideas. Such thoughts are part of a deadly scheme, the end of which is always death.

I can just hear some say, "She believes there exists an 'intelligence' behind evil? What is she, illiterate? This sounds like something out of *The Twilight Zone*."

In case you think I sound uncool, stop and consider. One glance at the track record of moral evil in this world's hall-of-history horrors should convince you that it smells of something systematized. And systems don't just happen. They are devised. They are schemed. Behind them is intelligence.

Judaism, Christianity, Buddhism, Islam—they all recognize an intelligence behind moral evil.

Little wonder that Jesus not only believed in a Devil but nailed him with the name "Tempter." Jesus called him that when the Devil enticed Him to stand on the highest point of the temple and throw Himself down.[1]

And the Tempter had one goal: murder. That's why, later on, Jesus nailed him again: "He was a murderer from the beginning, not holding to the truth, for there is no truth in him. When he lies, he speaks his native language, for he is a liar and the father of lies."[2]

The Tempter. Murderer from the beginning. Father of lies. The Devil's goal is to destroy your life, either by making your existence a living nightmare, or by pushing you into an early grave. Take heed: If you have ever been enticed to prematurely end your life, then you've been listening not just to something but to someone. And just what are a few of the tempting lies he whispers?

"No One Cares"

One afternoon a couple of weeks ago, I was sitting at my friend's coffee table, wrestling with whether or not I should tell her about the depression that had gripped me for several days. I decided to open up.

"Do you have time to listen?" I asked.

"Sure," she said, and promptly rose to retrieve a whistling teakettle from the stove. As she poured, I took a deep breath and started to unfold my problem.

Pause. "Milk in your tea?" Nod yes. Start again. Phone rings. "Wait a minute." Pick up where we left off. Knock at door. "What were you saying?" More distractions.

Friend half-listens. Friend gets up to warm tea. Help. I hurt. And this person could not care less.

C. Samuel Storms said,

> Beneath the waterline of every life are the frustrated longings, sinful schemes, thoughts and fantasies of a fallen soul . . . here are where people are hurting. Tragically, we rarely encounter one another at that level. . . . How adept we have become in our ability to get along without one another.[3]

It's true. Some people could care less. Friends get preoccupied . . . nurses rush by your bed to the next patient . . . neighbors never venture across the street to see how you're doing . . . families move apart and connect only occasionally over the phone.

In fact, you may feel no one cares about you. If so, those feelings might be justified. I've wheeled down nursing-home hallways, peered into rooms, and have grieved to see lonely people sitting and staring, waiting for someone to visit them. Or you may be a lonely person who rubs shoulders with plenty of people all the time but have no intimate contact with them. Discussion about weather and sports may fill your day, while the real issues, the kind that eat at you when you lie awake thinking at night, stay harbored inside. You think, *Does anyone care?*

There *are* people who care. And it's possible you have built a self-imposed wall around you, a wall that allows absolutely no one inside to see what you're going through and to hurt with your hurts.

Your Creator never intended that you should shoulder a load of suffering by yourself. That's the whole purpose of spiritual community—God deliberately designed people to need each other. We must rub shoulders with people of hope and faith if our innermost needs are to be met.

And what if your relationships with those few friends aren't as open or as dependable as you'd like them to be? Then it may be up to you to do something about it. A community of people who give the kind of love that "has its sleeves rolled up" can be created, if not found! A spontaneous, warm connection could develop with the chaplain in the hospital . . . a new friendship could happen with the kindly woman who visits your roommate . . . a fellowship could grow with those one or two people you always see praying in the hospital chapel . . . or maybe caring people could be found in that support group you've been avoiding.

That caring person may be a relative who is not so distant. An old friend you almost forgot about. A coworker who used to invite you to lunch now and then. People who care can be found in homeless shelters. In churches. At meetings of Alcoholics Anonymous. At

Parents Without Partners, Weight Watchers, and at handicap associations.

Someone cares. That fact was driven home when Terry Anderson, the American journalist held hostage for over six years, was released out of Lebanon. Isolated in a cell, blindfolded and abused, he had every reason to think that no one cared. But the few snippets of BBC broadcasts over which he heard his sister's voice were all he needed. Someone cared. And although he could only imagine his sister's embrace, he knew a friend was on the other side of his despair. That thought alone helped him get through.

"There's Nothing More to Expect from Life"

This is another standard lie, and it's a tempting thought, especially when you can't see beyond the thick, gray fog of hopelessness that has settled around you. But it is still a lie. There is life on the other side of that fog.

Viktor Frankl put it this way:

> In the concentration camp, I remember two cases of would-be suicide which bore a striking similarity. Both used the typical argument—they had nothing more to expect from life. In both cases it was a question of getting them to realize that *life was still expecting something from them* . . .
>
> For one, it was his child whom he adored . . . for the other it was a thing, not a person. This man was a scientist and had written a series of books which still needed to be finished. A man who becomes conscious of the responsibility he bears toward a human

being who affectionately waits for him, or to an unfinished work, will never be able to throw away his life. He knows the "why" for his existence and will be able to bear almost any "how."[4]

You may not be expecting anything from life, but life is still anticipating something from you. Like the man in the concentration camp, your responsibility may be to a child, perhaps to a grandchild or the young boy down the street. Your decision to die or not to die has a powerful impact on the mind of a boy or girl.

In the movie *The Boy Who Could Fly*, the father, who felt that he had nothing to give, ended his life prematurely, leaving two children. His son became withdrawn and sullen. Leaning on his elbows, the teary-eyed boy mumbled about his father's demise, "He didn't even try to fight . . . he just gave up . . . he didn't try." The father's decision had a lasting and negative impact on that child's life.

In a different example a friend of mine named Carol Swegle had everything: a rich husband, a beauty-queen title, a gorgeous country home, wealthy friends, and loving children. But Carol became depressed and tried to find relief in a combination of prescription drugs and alcohol. She had pinned all her hopes on a little bit of fame and a small fortune only to discover emptiness. One day in her bedroom, she placed a gun in her mouth and readied herself to pull the trigger. At that instant, her children burst into the room and startled her. The gun went off.

Carol fell to the floor, a quadriplegic. She lost her husband, her house, her friends, and ended up living in a nursing home. If ever there was a time to pull a trigger, it would have been then! But Carol hung on to the hope of claiming back her children. Her daughters gave her reason enough to try again. In the end? Although it was true that her children had been adversely affected by her suicide attempt, in the long run, through Carol's perseverance and changed attitude, her decision to live became her children's redemption. They were reunited.

Life, perhaps in a child, is still expecting something from you.

Then again, life, perhaps in a thing, is anticipating more from you. I receive letters from prisoners, disabled people in institutions, and elderly folks who often send poems, small paintings, crayoned drawings, crocheted bookmarkers, pot holders . . . whatever. These things are expressions of an individual to me, another person. Scribbled drawings and tattered bookmarks are expressions of the soul, and these simple things tie this person to the rest of the world.

"I Can't Live with This Depression"

You don't have to believe that lie. Admittedly, nothing distorts reality like depression. A blowup with your husband has you discounting twenty years of a good marriage. A little headache has you wondering if you've got brain cancer. A diagnosis of a serious illness has you digging your grave the next day. It's amazing how quickly reality gets turned upside down when you're depressed.

But I was impressed with the way this teenager approached her depression:

Dear Joni,

My name is Katherine and I'll be fourteen in four days. It also marks my first year in my wheelchair. I've lost the use of my legs and one arm forever. (The arm part is my own fault though.) I wouldn't do my therapy because I was so depressed over my bleak future.

Now I've discovered I need God's love more than ever. I want to start off talking with someone who knows what I'm going through. Please help me find the love a Christian knows.

Katherine is barely in her teens, has lived in a wheelchair for virtually a year, and yet devotes not more than one line to her depression. Most of us would devote an entire page!

When I wrote back to Katherine, I shared how even stained-glass-window saints, like the apostles, got depressed. The apostle Paul wrote to his friends in a letter,

> We are pressed on every side by troubles, but not crushed and broken. We are perplexed because we don't know why things happen as they do, but we don't give up and quit. We get knocked down, but we get up again and keep going.[5]

There's a little bit of that attitude in Katherine. Somehow after hitting rock bottom, she was able to get up again and keep going. I'm sure it took time to work through her sorrow, grief, and limitations, but somewhere in the fog of hopelessness, she found a thin ray of hope.

It's called faith. You don't need much more than the mustard-seed-sized faith of a fourteen-year-old girl. True,

Katherine, like most of us, will face even tougher times in the future, but she has begun to learn to choose her attitude and to invest her life in others. In so doing, she will be able to live, no matter what her feelings.

"Nothing Awaits Me After Death"

This could be the biggest lie of all.

And this is exactly why the Devil enjoys helping you scheme your own murder. Does that sound harsh? You may call it self-deliverance or euthanasia if you wish; it matters little to the Devil. It's all murder to him.

Also it matters little whether or not you believe in hell. Again the Devil doesn't care whether you label it "a white light at the end of a tunnel," or "nirvana," or "never-never land." It's all hell to him.

And what is it like? Fire and brimstone? A black hole? A bleak nothingness? Again the Devil shrugs his shoulders at such descriptions. All that matters to him is that hell is separation, total and final, from God. Hell is misery, more deep and profound than any misery you could experience on earth. And because misery loves company, the Devil wants to take as many with him to hell as he possibly can. That includes you.

Frankly it's enough that Jesus believed in hell, and he spoke of it more often than He did of heaven. Without going into a lot of detail here, Jesus simply warned, "It is better for you to enter life maimed or crippled than to have two hands or two feet and be thrown into eternal fire."[6]

The Tempter would have you believe that it's not that bad a place. And just how does the Devil beguile you into hell before you can find heaven? His strategy reminds me of a letter I read recently that described advice given to a man dying from AIDS:

Dear Editor,

A terminally ill AIDS patient recently called the Hemlock Society of North Texas. He was suffering greatly . . . in our phone conversations his anguish over the conviction that he would probably go to hell also came out.

I told him of my own and other beliefs, which differ greatly, on this subject. I described a recent survey that shows that about fifty percent of all Americans believe in the existence of hell, but only about four percent think they are likely to go there. With the help from my friendly local librarian, I obtained a copy of this survey to send him, along with the Drug Dosage Table of the National Hemlock Society.

This may be the first time the Society has helped someone to carry out a "double self-deliverance," both from a harsh terminal illness and from a harsh theological conviction.

The Hemlock Society of North Texas[7]

This person with AIDS was told the truth about how to kill himself with lethal drugs, but he wasn't told the truth about hell. The letter was an eerie cover-up of the facts. Do you believe that nothing awaits you after death? Would you be willing to stake your life on it? Of all the questions to be settled before you take the final exit, this issue is paramount.

If you think that hell is fiction, then say so. Don't be like the fifty percent of Americans who believe in hell but claim it's not their destiny. If you have even an inkling that it may be real, then wake up. Leave no stone unturned, no means untried until you find life worth living both on this side of eternity and on the other.

Don't Believe Lies

The Devil will go to any lengths to charm you into an early grave—everything from pushing drug dosage tables in your face, to pooh-poohing hell as pure nonsense. He'll move all of hell (and heaven if he could) to stop your heartbeat and have you pronounced dead.

Let's unmask his way of operating.

This morning I was having a rough start getting out of bed. My paralysis was giving me fits. I shook my head and growled, "This body is a pain. I hate it!"

Why was that so awful? Because the Enemy has a deep hatred of my body, and all I was doing was agreeing with him. He gets a charge out of my verbal barbs about my body. And he would like to get you to do the same. Whether you are approaching the final throes of a terminal illness, or whether you're deep in depression, the Devil delights in hearing us bad-mouth our bodies.

Why? Because your body, even underneath wrinkles or fat, and in spite of the ravages of illness or old age, is made in the image of God. Your heart, mind, hands, and feet are stamped with the imprint of the Creator. Little wonder the Devil wants you to do your body in!

This morning I had to plug my ears once again against the lies of the Tempter and remember that I am "fearfully and wonderfully made."[8] I rehearsed the old, familiar truth that God has a plan for this flesh and blood of mine. That's why the Devil considers my body a threat. He understands that when I yield to God my body, albeit paralyzed, my feet and hands are powerful weapons against his forces of darkness.

Listen to the Truth

By the way, the Devil would have you believe a couple of more lies. He wants to convince you that he is either a powerless elf-gone-bad in a red suit with a funny tail, or an evenly matched and almost-as-mighty opponent of God. Neither is true.

The Devil is only a fallen angel.[9]

He is a deceiver.[10]

He is doomed for destruction.[11]

And until then, he has one goal in mind: your destruction.

Discussion Guide

Liar, Liar. . .

Just this once, you get to practice lying. Consider the following situations and develop a lie that Satan would tell each person. Write the lie on the right-hand side.

Satan's Lie

- A teenage girl with cerebral palsy (a disability that can restrict motion and speech and physical appearance)
- A 40-year-old man with Down's syndrome (a form of mental retardation)
- An 80-year-old man in a nursing home
- Parents of a four-year-old son in a coma
- The disabled child of a parent who just filed for divorce

1. What is Satan's purpose in telling such lies?

2. Why does Satan want society to be deceived? What is the evidence that such deception has occurred?

3. What does the Bible say about defending ourselves and others against such lies?

7

Your Decision Matters to God

Some people would look at Diane Sabol sitting in her big, bulky wheelchair, stiff and motionless, and shake their heads. She has to be fed everything and pushed everywhere. The creeping limitations of her multiple sclerosis have curled her fingers, making them stiff and rigid. Her voice is barely a whisper. Often she has to stay in bed.

"Why doesn't she just end it all?" some people say. Diane struggled through the diagnosis of her disease, an ensuing divorce, and a custody battle for her children. Then she went through more paralysis and pain only to be forced by her MS to lose her children again. From there she went downhill to a lonely and dreary existence in an institution. "I didn't want to live to see my fortieth birthday," Diane recalls.

Things are much better now for Diane. Somewhere in the midst of hopelessness, Diane was able to connect with one or two nurse's aides. A fragile friendship slowly strengthened with one aide named Connie, and several years later, Diane was able to move into a small apartment with the help of her new friend. Diane saw Connie as an answer to prayer. In fact, she began to see that her life was worth living because of two things: people and God. "Now on this my fiftieth year of life, I'm looking forward to the years ahead," she told me recently.

Diane still spends all of her time either in her wheelchair or bed. Her paralysis is getting worse. Her vision is dimming. Yet Diane finds satisfaction in her work. In fact, others literally depend on her for finding life worth living. She spends hours at work, reaching out to the gangs in the streets of east L.A., aiding homeless mothers, single parents, abused children, despondent teenagers, and the dying and forgotten old people in the nursing home where she once lived. She works to move mountains that block the paths of Peace Corps workers in Latin America and help open the eyes of the spiritually blind in Southeast Asia.

No, Diane doesn't run a crisis hotline. Her telephone wires are invisible but no less real; and her work, although spiritual, is accomplishing just as much as if she were talking one-on-one with homeless mothers, gang members, and abused children. Diane's work is to pray.

This meek and quiet woman sees her place in the world; it doesn't matter that others may not recognize her significance in the grand scheme of things. Her motto? "The point of this life . . . is to become the person God can love perfectly, to satisfy His thirst to love. Being counts more than doing, the singer more than the song. We had better stop looking for escape hatches, for this is our hatchery."[1] "Finally," Diane says, "I've found peace."

Perhaps you're not slumped in a big, bulky wheelchair. You may not even be dying, debilitated, or terminally ill. But still you'd give anything to feel the peace Diane has found. Trouble is, you might be tempted to still believe the lie that peace is found by prematurely ending your life.

True, you may feel that no one seems to care. And maybe not a soul does care! You may feel as though life is not expecting a single thing from you, and you simply cannot live with depression. Sadly you are even willing to stake your life on the belief that nothing awaits you after death.

If so, you *need* peace! But remember, peace of mind comes not in the form of sentences but people. There is a Person who cares about you, even if no one else does. He calls Himself the Prince of Peace. And it is His perspective on life I want to talk to you about.

The Bible Speaks Out on Euthanasia

You may think that euthanasia of dying or debilitated people is a rather recent phenomenon, but not so. The Old Testament records an incident involving King Saul of Israel, who became seriously wounded on the battlefield. Fearing the advancing enemy, Saul took his own sword and tried to fall against it. He cried to a soldier, in effect, "Come and put me out of my misery for I am in terrible pain but life lingers on."

The soldier deferred to the wishes of the king and killed him. Then acting most likely on his innocence, he brought some of Saul's armor to David and said, "I killed him, for I knew he couldn't live."[2]

There were no laws on the books back then about assisted suicide, but that did not stop David from banging the gavel of Israel's justice. He ordered the soldier put to death. Perhaps onlookers were shocked by the verdict. After all, Saul was dying anyway, he was in great pain, and if captured, he feared torture and abuse in his final hours. These things were probably on the mind of the soldier who performed the mercy killing, but his actions stand in contrast with Saul's bodyguard who, minutes earlier, was too terrified to commit the act.[3]

To be fair, it seems that Saul's status as king of Israel added to the guilt of the deed, and David was outraged that someone had the nerve to harm the king who was anointed of God. But I believe it's fair to draw a principle that is as true for people today as for people living several thousand years ago. Whether a monarch or a common man, mercy killing anybody is wrong; Saul's being king only heightened the criminality of the soldier's deed.[4]

God clearly opposes *active euthanasia*, whether it be plunging a sword into the bleeding body of a king on a battlefield, or plunging a syringe full of phenobarbital into the veins of a dying patient. The prohibition against murder in the Ten Commandments logically includes murder of the self. Mercy killing and suicide contradict the legitimate self-love of "love your neighbor as *yourself*."[5]

As far as *passive euthanasia* is concerned, there's no biblical account of someone withdrawing medical treatment to cause death, an act that constitutes passive euthanasia. But it's not hard to imagine that had King Saul been rescued by paramedics and put on life supports, only to have some Amalekite unplug them, God would have frowned. Mercy killing, whether committed actively or passively, is always presented in a negative light in the Bible. In Scripture, people who either killed themselves or sought to be put out of their misery are always seen as disobedient.[6]

And as far as those who will say, "I'll do with my body as I wish," God has a response: "You are not your own. . . . Therefore honor God with your body."[7]

In short, any means to produce death in order to alleviate suffering is never justified. Or in the language of the Bible, it is never right to do evil.[8]

The Bible Speaks Out On Dying

However, *letting someone die* is another matter entirely. Allowing a person to die when he is, in fact, dying is justified. The Bible is full of examples of people doing all they can to help a person live, but when it came time to die, Scripture doesn't do much more than record the death. No paramedics called to the scene, no CPR, no Heimlich maneuver. The Old and New Testaments do not specifically address many of our present-day problems and questions related to "letting someone die." Scripture is probably silent because those problems didn't exist in biblical times. The absence of respirators, drug therapies, heart pumps, and feeding tubes did not confuse the difference between prolonging the process of dying and sustaining life.

In fact, the Bible speaks about death not in technical terms, but in the everyday language of ordinary experience. Today, doctors would agree a person is dead if the functions of the brain and brain stem cease, but Scripture does not formally define death in those terms or any others. It simply assumes we understand what death is.

But what Scripture lacks in absolute definitions, it makes up for in absolute decrees. There's a kind of medical dictionary exactness to a verse like Job 14:5, "Man's days are determined; you have decreed the number of his months and have set limits he cannot exceed."

Trade Fear In for Peace

People's intense interest in euthanasia can be summed up in one word: fear. Ever since the days of Eden, we've been haunted by fear of each side of the grave we look at. Like the old song goes, "I'm tired of living, but scared of dying." On this side of the tombstone, our fears are aggravated by strange new diseases, machines that dehumanize, and treatments that rob dignity. Yet peering beyond the tombstone, we're afraid of that scary left-turn into hell.

Peace is the opposite of fear. As I shared, we are all in search of peace when it comes to life-and-death decisions. And the Prince of Peace is the only one who can rid you of fear no matter which side of the grave you look at. The Bible calms our fears when it says:

"Since we, God's children, are human beings—made of flesh and blood—he also became flesh and blood by being born in human form; for only as a human being could he die and in dying break the power of the Devil who had the power of death. Only in that way could he deliver those who through fear of death have been living all their lives as slaves to constant dread."[9]

Read it again. God became a human being—that's Jesus. Jesus, through His death, broke the power of the Devil and his lies. He also wants to deliver you of your fears, whether fear of life as a living nightmare or fear of death as a permanent and total separation from God. To believe in Jesus gives you peace in the here and now and peace about the hereafter.

How? Well, remember that scary left-turn into hell? What makes it so foreboding is our guilt. And guilt is no psychological fiction: You've broken Somebody's law, and no matter how much others may flatter you on the outside, on the inside a guilty conscience nails you for lust, pride, and prejudice, just to name a few. The punishment for breaking the law is death. But like the verse says, Jesus *delivers!* When He bore God's punishment, Jesus raised His cross as a sign marker, arranging a right turn away from hell and into heaven.

To place your hand in the Prince of Peace's hand does not necessarily guarantee you protection from suffering, nor does it offer immunity from difficult deathbed-decisions. But it does give you a steadfast hand to hold on to, including the certainty that a loving and all-powerful God, who knows everything, is standing by your side. Putting your confidence in Christ will free you from living all your life as a slave to constant dread—dread of facing life as a living nightmare, and dread of facing death as the dark unknown.

God loves life; God despises death, for "the last enemy to be destroyed is death."[10] Jesus said, "My purpose is to give life in all its fullness"—life not only in the here and now, but in the hereafter.[11] There are good reasons why God wants you to live: He wants you to have peace, He knows your life can have value in the here and now, and He wants you to make that right turn into heaven.

God Knows You're Heading for a Hereafter

If you were to ask Diane Sabol which truth from the Bible gave her the most peace, she might say, "I consider that our present sufferings are not worth comparing with the glory that will be revealed in us."[12]

That's saying a mouthful! Some people find it difficult to think realistically about heaven. Even the spiritually minded feel awkward working toward "eternity" because it seems so far away, almost unreal. Even when we try to imagine what it would be like, we come up short of a real desire to go there. Who wants to live forever tucked behind a galaxy where birds chirp, organs play, and angels bounce from cloud to cloud?

If that were a true picture of heaven, an awful lot of people besides Diane would be lukewarm about going there.

The fact is, descriptions about heaven aren't as important as grasping the *fact* of heaven. Heaven is the place where God is going to give His family the biggest welcome-home party in history. Entrance into heaven means no more suffering, no more tears, and a life free from pain and filled with joy. Perhaps that's why people who are dying, debilitated, or terminally ill are often those most ready to believe in God. Maybe the Devil could care less about whether or not you believe in hell, but God definitely cares whether or not you believe in heaven! Your eternal destiny rests on it.

Believing in Jesus is the first step to a life that goes far beyond this world. Once that is settled, there are a few facts we can hold on to until we cross the other side of the grave and step into a brighter eternity with God.

You were made for one purpose, and that is to make God real to those around you. Don't think He has left you without any means whatever for fulfilling that end, just because you are confined to bed or struggling with pain. In a mysterious way each day that you live, each hopeful thought you think, however fleeting, each smile you muster brings God incredible joy. That's because your positive attitude and actions, however small and faint, are fingers pointing others to a God who is larger and finer and grander than they thought. That's what it means to glorify Him as you lie in that bed, sit in that wheelchair, or persevere through that depression.

Your suffering has meaning now and forever. This is what Diane's favorite verse is all about. Your present suffering isn't worth comparing with the glory that will be revealed in you. How can that be? Loneliness, feelings of total abandonment, pain, and the like are capable of being exchanged for something precious, eternal, weighty, and real—so much so that it's hardly worth comparing the two. God will one day reward you for sticking through suffering with an uncomplaining attitude. When you exchange your anger for faith in Him, then your life in heaven will be larger, finer, and grander because of that very suffering.

God works in your life up until the final moment. It may appear that nothing is taking place in the life of a dying loved one, a comatose individual, or a severely incapacitated person, but God is not hindered from accomplishing His work in a life just because it seems nothing is happening. The work of God is spiritual activity, often far separate from one's brain, neurological, or muscular activity. Only eternity will reveal the work that was accomplished.

Dying is your final passage. The stripping of all human powers, mental as well as physical, is a part of the process that George MacDonald calls "undressing for the last, sweet bed." When we who believe in God die, we leave behind our permanent claim on our earthly "clothes" and we are "clothed upon" with immortality.[13]

God knows you're heading for a hereafter. For those who, apart from Him, prematurely end their lives hoping to find relief, there will only be a hereafter of vast and utter disappointment. For those who believe in Jesus, the dying process becomes the most significant passage of their lives. Theirs is a hereafter of more joy than they can possibly imagine.

God Knows and Wants You Here and Now

I once cornered Dr. J. I. Packer, a prominent evangelical theologian, and asked him this question: "What would you suggest to a severely handicapped man with cerebral palsy who was totally bedridden, nonverbal, and relegated to a back bedroom in a nursing home? No one visits him and no nurse takes time to benefit from his good attitude. What can that handicapped man do?" I knew plenty of real-life examples, so the question wasn't hypothetical.

Dr. Packer folded his hands, thought for a moment, and then replied, "A man like that can worship and glorify God."

That response almost sounded as though Dr. Packer were piously patting the handicapped man on the head and trivializing his plight with a platitude that was too heavenly minded. But I've encountered enough handicapped people, just like the man with cerebral palsy, to know that Dr. Packer is right, and I've looked long enough into the Bible to know his advice is well-taken.

I think of Tracy Traylor, a beautiful blonde-haired college student who suffered a severe head injury and was in a coma for five and one-half months. She came out of it unable to walk or talk well enough for people outside her family to understand her.

I met Tracy and her mother at a conference. Tracy, sitting slumped in her wheelchair, slightly lifted her bobbing head and shoved something in her lap toward me. It was a necklace made of clay and colored beads, and one of the clay pieces had an imprint of a leaping deer.

"Oh Tracy," I said, "this is beautiful. Thank you for the gift."

"My daughter was a design student in college and she directs me on how to craft each piece of jewelry," her mother proudly explained. I could hardly imagine the enormous effort it took for the two of them to communicate.

Just then I noticed a verse typed on a piece of paper twist-tied to the necklace. It was Isaiah 35:4, 6, "Your God will come . . . Then will the lame leap like a deer." I couldn't hold back the tears. Although Tracy couldn't speak, her smile spoke volumes. Her brilliant and shining hope cast shadows on me. I glanced around at the hundreds of people who were rushing by us, each of them oblivious to the powerful message of the college girl in her wheelchair.

Maybe millions of people could care less about this girl's lovely attitude, but Someone far more significant cared, and He had a purpose. "The purpose is that all the angelic powers should now see the complex wisdom of God's plan being worked out through the church."[14]

Whether a godly attitude shines from a brain-injured college student or from a lonely man relegated to a back bedroom, the response of patience and perseverance counts. God points to the peaceful attitude of suffering people to teach others about Himself. He not only teaches those we rub shoulders with every day, but He instructs the countless millions of angels and demons. The hosts in heaven stand amazed when they observe God sustain hurting people with His peace.

It matters to God not only *that* you live but *how* you live.

God Can Be Trusted Even When There Are No Reasons

The message was scribbled and rain splattered: "Laurel Ledford needs to talk to you." We met in an office at the retreat center where I was speaking. I was surprised when she entered the room carrying her three-month-old baby. It was cold and windy, not the kind of day you would take an infant outside. But, then again, it wasn't easy for Laurel to find someone to baby-sit her son with spina bifida. She sat across from me in a heavy sweater, holding her handicapped child bundled in blankets.

Laurel relayed her story, one incident after another of heart-twisting disappointment. First they moved, after selling all they had, so her husband, Steve, could go to school. Then they had one child named Stephen. Next she carried and lost a baby girl. Then another. Immediately after the loss of her second child, she accidentally became pregnant. When she was six months along, her husband had surgery, which further drained their already limited bank account.

She tugged at her little boy's blanket and in tears, said, "I thought I could handle losing another baby, but I could definitely not handle a baby with a birth defect. Shortly after that, my doctor told me that the baby I was carrying had severe hydrocephalus and spina bifida. He told me that one option would be to have a spontaneous delivery."

"You mean abortion?"

Laurel nodded. I mentally added the phrase "spontaneous delivery" to that list of pleasant-sounding euphemisms.

"But I would *not* choose to lose my baby," she said. "Still that's when depression and thoughts of suicide came to mind. I spent a long, gray midwestern winter on the couch watching a lot of TV."

Laurel went on to say that after the birth of David, her baby with spina bifida, she struggled with more feelings of hopelessness. "David's head size looked terrible, and I was struggling with bonding. I didn't want him or even like him. I had so much guilt and confusion—"

I had to interrupt. "What kept you going?"

Laurel hiked David on her lap to think. "I plastered our walls with Scriptures. Psalm 34:18 says, 'The Lord is close to the brokenhearted and saves those who are crushed in spirit.'" Then she paused for another long moment. "But sometimes I still get so depressed. There's no rhyme or reason for why all these awful things have happened."

She had a point. Any information I might have given Laurel at that moment would have come off sounding like clichés; sometimes the magnitude of a person's suffering seems to outweigh any potential benefit. The puzzle of suffering doesn't always get completed. Sometimes there are no reasons that satisfy. As Laurel pressed her lips to the bulging forehead of little David, I thought of a verse from Deuteronomy 29:29, "The secret things belong to the Lord our God."

"Joni," Laurel said, startling me from my thoughts. "How do I face tomorrow?" Her brown eyes looked so pleading.

I took a deep breath. "I have to confess I wonder the same thing. I get weak-kneed thinking about living another twenty-five years in a wheelchair. But God does not expect me to accept what may or may not happen to me twenty years from now."

Laurel gave a questioning look.

"God doesn't give strength to face next year's headaches or even next month's heartaches. He won't even loan you enough strength to face tomorrow. He only gives you and I strength to face today. To live one day at a time."

She nodded, as if understanding.

"I'm sure that's why Jesus said, 'Do not worry about tomorrow, for tomorrow will worry about itself. Each day has enough trouble of its own.'[15] You'll have to face tomorrow, Laurel, without answers to your questions. The best you and I can do is hold on to the One who holds the answers."

We spent the rest of our time together in silence, mostly listening to David breathe softly and sigh every once in a while. We both sensed that enough words had been spoken. Yet in the quiet a bond was growing between us. After a while, we hugged and said good-bye.

A month or so later I received a letter from Laurel. Life had not gotten easier. One evening her older boy Stephen disappeared. She was sick with panic. Neighbors were telephoned, the police were contacted, a search began. When Laurel heard the patrol car calling in the K-9 unit, she fell apart. "It was as if a demon were screaming into my ears, 'Do it now! Kill yourself! Shove your wrists through the front window!'"

A half hour later her son was found. He had been hiding in the house the whole time.

Why? What reasons could there possibly be for the torment and pain? There's no answer. But I noticed a P.S. at the close of her letter, a message that was better than any answer: "I'm trying to reach out to at least one person a day and do something for them that counts for eternity. It works!"

Your Decision Matters to a Personal God

Laurel heard the Devil screeching in her ear one moment and God whispering in her other ear the next. Should she shut her ears to the Devil's lies, or against God's words? Laurel teeters almost daily on the edge of eternity—that's why she sees every day as a choice. And her decision goes far beyond whether or not she should "Do it! Do it! End your life!"

Laurel, and many like her who have been tempted to leapfrog all the suffering, grit their teeth and decide daily to live. For these friends, life has value now and value in the hereafter.

It's something they remind themselves of each day. It's a decision they act on, a decision that matters to God.

Discussion Guide

In Heaven's Eyes

In the last segment you spent time lying. Now you get to be a reporter for heaven! On the left are hypothetical headlines from planet earth. Opposite each of earth's headlines, write a contrasting headline of victory from heaven's perspective for *Heaven's Hope*, the angels' daily newspaper.

Earth's Gazette	*Heaven's Hope Headlines*
Supreme Court upholds assisted suicide as constitutional	Assisted suicide declared a passing fad as thousands of Christians provide friendships and assistance to disabled people
First 24-hour euthanasia clinic opens in Toledo	
Abortion named as the number-one reason for dramatic decline in children born with disabilities	
Thousands of disabled denied health care by the Health Rationing Committee	

1. Consider the following scenario.

    Barbara is a young Christian who is in the last stages of Lou Gehrig's disease. She is totally paralyzed and, for her, the next step will be a ventilator to aid her in breathing. She wants to do what God wants but is unsure whether or not to get "hooked up."

    What would you tell her?

2. Have you ever had to trust God when there seemed to be no reasons for the crisis you were facing? What was it that brought you through?

PART THREE

—

You Can Have the Mind of Christ

8

IT'S TIME TO DECIDE

Hospital waiting rooms are like islands of refuge for many people. It is where the pastor comes to pray with you. Or where you flip open to just the right verse in the Bible prior to hearing the latest doctor's report: "I will not be afraid" the verse says. No one bothers you on the telephone. Strangers who occupy the room with you become fast friends, sharing the horror stories, then your backgrounds, and then your deepest fears. The room becomes a place to reflect on decisions made and choices yet to come.

We've been in the waiting room together these last seven chapters, getting accustomed to the language of the life-and-death dilemma, hearing what some in society are calling valid reasons for letting go and learning God's heart about the choices you must make. I wish we could stay longer, but you *must* make choices, you know. You weren't meant to stay in this waiting room forever. It's time to decide.

How you decide is the focus of this chapter. General guidelines are provided for all three dilemmas we've studied—death, health, and disability. And because each dilemma is unique, I also present specific principles that you can follow. These can, if considered in light of God's standards of measure, enable you to practice godly wisdom with peace and strength.

Seek good and godly advice. Your process of making personal decisions is as close as your doctor, family, and clergy. Insight for making distinctions can be drawn from the experience of a caring physician, the condition of the dying person, and the input of the family and religious counselors. Historically, life-and-death decisions have always been made this way. "In the multitude of counselors there is safety"[1] and wisdom is gathered from a physician who knows the facts, a patient who has expressed his wishes, a family who is looking out for their loved one first and foremost, and a pastor who can give godly guidance.

A good relationship between physician, patient, family, and pastor can be the wellspring of wisdom. But underline the word *relationship*. Unfortunately the care, trust, and confidence that once earmarked the fraternity between a doctor and the patient and a family has been replaced by new industry standards. The doctor has now become a health-care provider who offers a paid service to us, the consumers. It's rare to find physicians and families that build their relationship on trust, time, and commitment. And trust, plus an up-close and personal relationship, is needed to discern what is best for a dying family member.

A Christian has a unique privilege when it comes to making decisions. God places us in His kingdom as priests.[2] We are equipped to exercise God's will on earth. But we are not just priests. We are part of a priest*hood*. This means we belong to the church, Christ's living body. There are other priests who can collectively make a decision and to whom you can appeal in your dilemma.

Not only are we a part of a priesthood, God has ordained that within the priesthood of believers there be people who serve as shepherds. These shepherds are elders and pastors. You can not only seek their advice, you can ask them to govern your decision. You can submit yourself to their authority. There is much biblical precedence for such a thing. Paul submitted himself to the elders in Jerusalem. Hebrews 13:17 says, "Obey your leaders and submit to their authority. They keep watch over you as men who must give an account."

Our independent society is not comfortable with that kind of submission, but do not spurn it. There is great benefit for you, as I firmly believe that a dilemma, brought to elders in sincerity of motives, can be submitted to their collective judgment. Their decision, guided by the Holy Spirit, can serve as protection for you. God will not hold you accountable for your following the dictates of their Spirit-guided wisdom.

Don't make a cookie-cutter decision. It would be nice if we could look to decisions made by others and follow their recipe. But each situation has different nuances, and so great care must be taken not to imitate. My dad's story, for example, may or may not apply to your situation.

My dad was a rugged outdoorsman, but a series of strokes left him virtually bedridden. It was the long-feared nightmare that we, while growing up, always pushed from our minds. Our ninety-year-old Dad was but a shadow of his former self. His withered, bony frame could not hide the undaunted spirit that twinkled from his blue eyes, and it crushed our hearts to think that Daddy was probably going to die within a year, maybe months, or even weeks.

The family house in Maryland was sold. Mother moved herself and Dad to Florida, where he resided in a cheery, little nursing home. Mom walked from my uncle's house to the nursing-home every morning to care for her husband's needs and then returned at night after he was put to bed. My sisters and I often visited, and Linda, Jay, and Kathy most frequently stretched their visits so they could help our mother and dad.

Then, in a span of fewer than two weeks, everything changed. My father quickly began to fail. He was rushed to the hospital, and an IV was inserted. The tube was later removed when his body bloated and lungs filled. He was sent back to the nursing home. Our family collapsed in exhaustion. We agonized and conferred with doctors. After much prayer and painful discussion, we made a decision: no feeding tube.

It was clear that Daddy was dying, and knowing my father, we had no doubt that he would not want the process of his dying prolonged. My sisters and mom tenderly cared for Daddy around the clock during his last days, camping on couch pillows by his bedside and giving him what little water he could take.

Within days I received a phone call from Jay. Daddy had passed away. I sat for a long moment and then put my thoughts on paper.

In that little nursing home, my mother had sat vigil with Dad for over a year and a half, helping him daily and spreading the joy of the Lord to every elderly person up and down each hallway. In this last week, I joined my sisters and Mom there. It was obvious that Dad was failing fast. I had to leave after a few days—it was a tearful departure, knowing I'd never see my father again this side of eternity. But now, just days later, they called to say how Dad had turned to my mother, opened both his blue eyes for the first time in days, gave her a big, full smile, and languished for a moment in what they emphatically described as a "glow." It must have been the glow of God's presence because then . . . he passed away.

My mother, sisters, a recreational therapist, and a nurse held hands around his bed and sang a doxology. From there, my sisters canvassed the hallways, telling people, "Daddy just went to heaven to be with the Lord . . . isn't that exciting?"

I share that story because the process and the end result were such a positive experience that people might be tempted to try to duplicate it. But remember, God gives *necessary* wisdom for a *particular* problem—yours. Custom-fitted wisdom is needed for discerning particular life-or-death distinctions. And because it involves the life and death of a warm-blooded human being, each distinction is subjective, definitely not objective. Every situation is different; every person is unique.

So when it comes to the "pull the plug" question, don't waste your time looking for rules one-two-three and a tidy list of do's and don'ts. My family couldn't superimpose on Dad the experience of other families in that nursing home. In the same way, you can't take my family's decision and overlay it like a template on your family's situation. It doesn't work that way. Even Dr. Koop has said, "There is no way that there can be a set of rules to govern this circumstance. Guidelines may be possible, but not rules."[3]

Don't make any decision if you are depressed. So much of what is frightening about the modern-day trend toward euthanasia and assisted suicide is that people are making decisions about themselves and their family member while in a state of depression. Life-and-death decisions and depression are always deadly combinations. Depression will put a negative spin on everything. You won't see that your friends do care. You won't see the potential for a glorious outcome. You won't see the long-term consequences of your choice.

If you are in a state of depression, throw yourself into the arms of your friends and don't let go until you can say with the psalmist, "Why are you downcast, O my soul? Why so disturbed within me? Put your hope in God, for I will yet praise him, my Savior and my God."[4]

Pray. How trite that advice can seem, standing alone as it does in so many "how to" books and sermons. Were it not for its revolutionary and supernatural effect, I would not offer it as a guideline. But God listens. And God also speaks and imparts wisdom. Remember the injunction of James: "But if any of you lacks wisdom, let him ask of God." No decision you make in this life-and-death dilemma will be accompanied by peace unless you pray. Ask God in humility, at every turn. He'll be there, and as many have found, the dilemma you face now will in the days ahead, be a time of your greatest spiritual growth.

‑‑

The preceding guidelines apply to all three dilemmas we have examined. Each dilemma, however, carries with it some unique approaches.

At Death's Door

God is equipping you to make a godly choice at an incredible time. To help you discern His will, the following guidelines are helpful.

Determine whether or not you are sustaining life or prolonging death. Is it wise, for example, to pump up a person who is in the final death throes with more treatments and machines? Of course not. Dying begins when a person rapidly and irreversibly deteriorates, a person for whom death is imminent, a person who is beyond reasonable hope of recovery. Such people have a right to not have death postponed.

The line of distinction is not so much between life and death, as it is between life and dying. There are pages in medical dictionaries devoted to defining imminent death, but because the people who are "imminently dying" are unique, warm-blooded human beings in unique circumstances, it's impossible to pin down exactly when the process of dying begins. The International Anti-Euthanasia Task Force says that true, imminent death spans a period of days, perhaps hours. However, courts in some states widen the span of imminent death to a matter of weeks, and some say months! That's why a good relationship with your family's doctors is so critical. You need to get as close to the facts as possible.

There's a point, though, when it is futile and even burdensome to go into a full-court press against death, using every last bit of high-tech heroic treatment available. Dr. Koop advises,

> If someone is dying and there is no doubt about that and you believe as I do that there is a difference between giving a person all the life to which he is entitled as opposed to prolonging the act of dying, then you might come to a time when you say this person can take certain amounts of fluid by mouth and we're not going to continue this intravenous solution because he is on the way out.[5]

There are situations where giving food or water, whether by mouth or by tube feeding, is futile and excessively burdensome. Rita Marker of the International Anti-Euthanasia Task Force says,

> A patient who is very close to death may be in such a condition that fluids would cause a great deal of discomfort or may not be assimilated by his body. Food may not be digested as the body begins "shutting

down" during the dying process. There comes a time when a person is truly, imminently dying.[6]

The Christian Medical Society affirms that, "in exceptional cases, tube feeding may actually result in increased patient suffering during the dying process."[7]

If your loved one is not imminently dying, your decision to provide medical care will be beneficial. It will sustain his or her life to fulfill whatever God's purpose might be. If, however, you are desperately clinging to every medical procedure to delay death, then you are denying God's work. "It could be viewed as unethical . . . Extraordinary efforts to fight the divinely appointed limits of our mortality are really working in opposition to God."[8]

Provide comfort and relief from pain. The passing away of my father taught my family about finding wisdom in helping my dad live and letting him die. Giving food to the hungry and water to the thirsty is a requirement of basic decency. And even when it was clear that my father had entered that irrevocable process of death, we wanted to make him as comfortable as possible. This is part of the revealed wisdom of God that mandates compassionate care. Such compassion and decency was lived out poignantly as Kathy, Jay, and my mother moistened Dad's lips with ice chips, helped him sip juice when he was able, and even clear broth when possible.

By the way, had my father needed extraordinary amounts of pain medication, our family and doctors would have done whatever was necessary to make him comfortable. As it was, my father was comfortable without medication, but Proverbs 31:6–7 makes a strong case for strong analgesics, "Give beer to those who are perishing, wine to those who are in anguish; let them drink and forget their poverty and remember their misery no more." In the context of Proverbs, wine is a bad and deceitful thing, but in these two verses, its anesthetic and analgesic qualities are commendable for those who are dying or "in anguish."

Be an advocate for those in a coma or persistent vegetative state. Sometimes letters say it all. Like this one from the mother of a boy named Jeremy:

> Dear Joni,
>
> Our twelve-year-old child, Jeremy, was critically injured in an automobile accident in 1986. He lived but remained in a comatose state—we later learned that Jeremy was in a "locked in" condition, unable to open his eyes or speak. He was well-nourished through a feeding tube.
>
> We didn't think we could communicate with Jeremy. But after two years of hard work, physical therapy, God's grace, and money, one day it happened: When I put a softball under his hand, he very slightly moved his thumb for yes and his little finger for no. Our precious son suffered much during two-and-one-half years, and then the Lord took him home shortly before his fifteenth birthday. God used Jeremy's dark valley to point others to him.
>
> Patty Cabeen

Jeremy's story is inspiring yet sad. He represents thousands who are in permanent comas or vegetative states. Many of these are said to be hopelessly beyond recovery. Ultimately, that means they are in danger of losing personhood (and all the rights that go with being a person, including the right to life).

It is precisely these people in permanent comas or in PVS around which the right-to-die debate is really raging. These are the ones most at risk; these are the ones who are in danger of losing their lives. "The persistent vegetative state is being used as the hard case in order to get people used to the idea that there are some in our society whose lives aren't worthwhile, who can be terminated," says Dr. William Burke, a professor of neurology at St. Louis University.[9]

People in comas or PVS are the ones who, more often than not, have never made clear their wishes about respirators or feeding tubes. And their families are the ones most burdened and distressed. We can hardly imagine the pain, the financial crunch, the tears, trauma, and heartache they must endure.

These mothers and fathers, and husbands or wives, are placed in the awkward position of speaking on behalf of the person in PVS or a coma. And often, health-care professionals and the courts veto the family's directives. There are even cases where the family vetoes the doctor's directives, and the courts veto everybody's directives!

The question is usually: Why can't we let this person die?

It is at this exact point that I firmly pull on my hat as a disability advocate. People in comas or persistent vegetative states or even locked-in conditions, much like Jeremy's, are not dying (although Jeremy eventually died of complications); they are severely disabled. Sure, underline the word *severely* because some of these people can't swallow, others can. Some make movements that are intentional, others reflexive. Because they are nonverbal, they depend on the sensitive interpretations of their caregivers, just as the mother of a newborn can sense differences in a whimper. And some even dramatically recover after spending years in a coma or vegetative state.

But all things considered, they are disabled. And no matter how severe their handicapping condition, people are entitled to treatment and care. Perhaps their biggest handicap is that they are "socially disabled," unable to relate to people around them. They are further socially disabled because public sentiment is most often behind their stressed-out families. But people like Jeremy are still persons. And each one has a soul, a spirit.

I will not take time to elaborate on the right-to-die debate swirling around these people and their parents, husbands, or wives, since others have written exhaustively on it. But there is one perspective about an individual in a long-term coma or PVS that I rarely hear: *The Spirit of God is able to work dramatically in the spirit of such a person, perhaps more so than at any other time in his life.*

It may appear that nothing is taking place in the life of a man or woman in a coma or vegetative state, but remember that the work of God is spiritual activity, often very separate from a person's intellect or even basic brain activity. I know of people who have lain in bed for years, unable to relate. I also know of friends or family members who have sat at their bedsides and prayed, read Scripture or poetry, played inspirational music, laughed and loved with them. And I know that many of these people have come out of their sleep having connected with God in an extraordinary way.

How does that happen? Jesus said, "[Spiritual revelations are] not revealed to you by man, but by my Father in heaven."[10] And God can definitely work in the lives of people who have no intellectual capacity. Just look at the example of John the Baptist. While he was yet in his mother's womb, he leaped for joy.[11] Obviously, God did not need the brain of that baby in order to make Himself known. What a profound thought: God may not require a mind through which to reveal Himself!

This is good news for people who don't have a high IQ. It's good news for the child or adult who is mentally retarded. And this is probably the only and best good news for the more than ten thousand people in this country who are in comatose states. I am convinced that God does not need their brains, whether injured or traumatized, to reveal His truth.

And what happens when that time comes for the person in a coma or PVS to depart this earth? How can a family member rest in the knowledge that their loved one has made that right turn into heaven? As Dr. John Frame of Westminster Theological Seminary concludes, "You simply commend the person to God's mercy. Can a person be saved by God's grace in the moments of unconsciousness preceding death? Certainly."[12]

Admittedly, a truckload of arguments for "pulling the plugs" of respirators or feeding tubes can be stockpiled against the needs of people in comas or vegetative states: medical expenses, quality of life, family stress, patient suffering, the precedence of court rulings, and the pressure from the public. But it is for these very reasons that we should "Stop evaluating by what the world thinks about them or by what they seem to be like on the outside," as it says in 2 Corinthians 5:16 (TLB).

Such arguments, convincing as they may be, would dictate that it's reasonable to remove life-support systems—in spite of the fact that to do so would be active euthanasia. Rather, people like Jeremy need to be regarded from a transcendent and eternal view. "For what is seen is temporary, but what is unseen is eternal."[13]

Err on the Side of Life. The preceding guidelines should help you face the dilemma of death. But if after all is said and done you still have doubts, consider one last safeguard: Err on the side of life. Choose life, and no matter how murky the dilemma might be, your sincere doubt and your godly motive will hold you through the consequences. God will not reproach you for such an error.

I Want to Get Well

The dilemma of health has so many facets, even guidelines may seem distant and of little help. But I think the following provide a structure in which you can make a godly decision.

Evaluate what you want to accomplish. It is easy to get caught up in the medical profession's definition of what is best for a patient. So before getting on to the assembly line of health care you need to decide what you want. Do you want one hundred percent recovery at any cost? Do you want to be restored to your former level of activity, or are you willing to accept less ability? How long do you want to be engaged in the battle for health? These are the kinds of questions you might need to ask.

Consider the risks. People on the sidelines assume that the fear of further injury or death should play no part in your decision. "Go for it," they might encourage, taking no thought as to who will go under the knife! It's your body, however, and the risks associated with any medical decision should be considered. Ask the doctor just how "experimental" the procedure is. What are the side effects of this or that medication? What is the track record with other patients undergoing the same procedure?

Once having answered these questions, weigh the risk of doing something against doing nothing at all. Ask God for insight on which alternative carries the best means of achieving your health care objective.

Count the cost. Every health decision has consequences beyond our bodies. Your decision will have an impact on your family. How are they facing this crisis? What impact will further treatments or surgery have on your relationship with your spouse? Your decision will affect your emotional state. Are you prepared emotionally and spiritually to undergo the next step? Your decision will affect your finances. Have you prayed about how God will provide?

Seek second opinions. Everyone knows you can get a second opinion, but some people feel hesitant. They feel that perhaps they would violate the relationship with their doctor or somehow "hurt" his feelings. While it is nice of people to be so concerned, don't forget whose body it is you're talking about. Doctors are second-guessed all the time. It comes with the territory. And rather than hurting their feelings, a second opinion might even confirm the original diagnosis and treatment, thereby making your decision even easier.

Steve and Laurel Ledford are good examples of how to apply the preceding guidelines. Within a year after David's birth, it became apparent that his head would remain enlarged in the traditional hydrocephalic look. They knew that surgery was available to correct the problem. They also learned that correcting the problem would relieve pressure on the brain and could enhance David's mental development. Steve and Laurel asked God for specific direction and were able to answer questions to their satisfaction:

- The surgery would achieve the objective of giving David the best chance of fitting in with other kids and developing mentally.
- The potential for success outweighed the chances of further injury or death.
- They asked very specific questions of doctors and got second opinions.
- David would experience a little suffering but would recover relatively quickly after surgery.

- Financial resources were available through insurance.
- And the family was behind the idea.

The health care decisions Steve and Laurel made, though stressful, were made with a great deal of peace. David had his surgery. The jury is still out on the prognosis, but the family is confident that they made the right choice.

Disability Is Not the End

My list of modern-day heroes might look very much like yours—Corrie ten Boom, Billy Graham, Brother Andrew. However, having met thousands of disabled people and families of disabled people, I have heroes you may not have considered. There are people living in the trenches every day with disabling conditions—who face incredible odds. I've met moms and dads who spend hours and hours breaking their backs and sometimes their hearts, caring for a child. And I could hug every spouse who has hung in there with a disabled husband or wife.

These heroes are applying the following kinds of guidelines on a daily basis.

Set a standard of involvement. Whether you are disabled or have a disabled family member, you need to set your sights on access. Seek out as much access into the mainstream of life as is possible. Whether it is education or employment, hope for and act on the best. Though it may mean extra work, join activities at church, such as the church picnic. Or join the museum trip with others in the class, even if the building is terribly inaccessible or transportation hard to find. Even consider volunteering your services in some way, no matter how limited your abilities might be.

Access to all of life is a legal right, but it still remains the responsibility of each disabled person and his or her family to "go through the door." Such an approach to life will allow you to use your talents. It will keep your disabled brother from being sheltered and hidden at home. And it will mean added blessings to those around your Down's syndrome child when they experience his love.

Don't isolate yourself. Independence is an achievement dependent upon hard work and other people. The dilemma of disability, and the years of work associated with it, cannot be faced alone. Other people's involvement is a necessity. Consider starting a circle of friends who will be available to help with matters like transportation, shopping, respite care, and financial management. Such a circle of friends can not only help you make decisions in a crisis, but they can also relieve the physical and emotional burdens as well. Just think of how much such a circle would help Debbie whom we introduced in the first chapter.

Keep your promises. The divorce rate among families whenever there is a disabled member is about eighty percent. Four out of five marriages end in divorce! It's not surprising, given the physical and emotional strain. Many spouses are walking out because they've not been able to cope. People facing the dilemma of disability need desperately to cling to their vows "in sickness and in health, for better or for worse." Consider the impact on a disabled child as he or she sees a parent leave. No matter how much Mom and Dad say, "It's not your fault," the child believes it to be true. Unlike a divorce over finances or infidelity, a divorce in this case is related directly to the disabled child.

A facility versus my home. I include this rather specific subject because it concerns so many people. Unfortunately, there is a great amount of pain and guilt being felt over this issue. Families would do well to talk about the subject before the day comes when it is forced on them.

When at all possible, a person will much prefer staying at his or her own home or at the home of a loved one. Such a desire is to be expected. Some children or spouses can provide needed care. Home health-care nurses can also help persons achieve their goal of staying at home.

Sometimes the degree of care exceeds what either a family member or a home health-care nurse can provide. At such times, everyone must focus on what would be best for the parent or spouse and make a decision that might include placement in a residential facility. If a decision is made based purely on convenience, however, you are missing a wonderful opportunity for God to minister to your family. A decision of convenience also deprives the elderly person of the honor he or she deserves.

If a decision is made to place a person in a facility, do not forget that the family can still practice "homeness." That means you should try to use as much time and creativity as you apply at home to make the person feel loved. Nursing homes are full of residents whose families make the obligatory Sunday afternoon visit. *Find time throughout the week to visit.* Have parties. Let them dictate a letter. Check closely on the care they are receiving. Or simply sit and stroke their hand or sing a song.

It's Your Choice

I hope you have sensed my caution in how you make your decisions in the life-and-death dilemmas. I am cautious because so many in our society today are not. They escape at the first sign of trouble and then claim it as their constitutional right.

Although I am cautious, I am not sitting back on my hands. Life-and-death dilemmas can be thrust upon a person at any moment. That is why my husband, Ken, and I have planned ahead for that time when we will have to make choices.

Discussion Guide

Guidelines, Not Prescriptions

Using the guidelines presented in chapter 8, discuss the following scenarios. Be sure to point out which guideline(s) you used in making the decision.

Richard, a strong Christian, is a seventy-six-year-old man who, in the last twenty years, has dealt with a mild form of diabetes. Lately, his diabetic condition has become aggravated due to changes in his diet and encroaching age. His family has been told that Richard needs to undergo a limb amputation to safeguard his health. His family wants him to proceed with the operation, but Richard would rather not. As Richard's younger brother, what would you advise? What guidelines would you communicate?

Susan, not a Christian, has full-blown AIDS and has contracted several infections whose combined impact has weakened her condition. She has an option of enlisting in a new drug-treatment program but lately has become weary of the tireless efforts of her Christian friends to keep her alive. She would like to check herself into a hospice and give up the fight. If you were her Christian friend, what would you do? What guidelines would you apply?

Harold, a young, athletic man, just received news from his doctor that he has lymphoma. This has plummeted him into depression, since he has also gone through a recent divorce. Harold has flatly told his doctor that he does not want the cancer treated at all. How would you help Harold if you were the doctor? What guidelines would you use?

Jeannie, when she was a teenager, was affected in her shoulder by polio. She now is suffering post-polio syndrome and is experiencing difficulty in breathing. Her husband is especially concerned at night when Jeannie is asleep, and he fears that she may be suffering from oxygen depletion. She is able to walk and can move her polio-affected arm and shoulder slightly. She's not sure if she wants to walk around the rest of her life with a portable ventilator. What would you tell her if you were her best friend? What guidelines would you share?

Your ninety-two-year-old father has suffered a series of strokes and has been bedridden for several years. His condition just took a turn for the worse, and he is not able to swallow. The doctor placed him on an IV, but his body seems to be bloated as a result of the fluid. Your main concern is that he be made comfortable. What should you do? What guidelines would you apply?

1. How would you classify someone in a permanent vegetative state? Are they still a person? Read the following statement by a medical ethicist.

> . . . Those operating within a Christian-belief system may be attracted to the conclusion that death is the total and irreversible loss of the capacity to participate in God's creative and redemptive purposes for human life. For it is reasonable for Christians to believe that it is precisely this capacity that endows

human life with its special significance. More specifically, this is the capacity to shape an eternal destiny by means of decision-making and soul-making, requiring as it does, both spiritual agency and spiritual receptivity—all of which presuppose conscious existence (that is "psychic" life) and not mere organic functioning (that is, somatic life). Indeed, it is reasonable to suppose that human organic life has no value in its own right but receives its significance from the fact that it can make possible and sustain personal consciousness and thereby make possible the capacity to participate in God's creative and redemptive purposes.

The same point can be made by putting matters in a slightly different way. When an individual becomes permanently unconscious, the person has passed out of existence, even if biological life continues.

Robert Wennberg from *Terminal Choices*

Do you agree with his evaluation that a permanently unconscious person has lost personhood? Why or why not?

9

ENDING WELL

"If I expect life to be unending, then dying seems to be an illusion. If I live life as a vocation, then dying is an intrusion. If life is a threat, then dying is an escape. If I accept life as a gift, then dying is a part of the given."[1]

Ben Coombs, an estate planner and a friend from my church, pulled up a chair next to my desk, opened his briefcase, and spread before me a four-page form titled "Durable Power of Attorney for Health-Care Decisions." It explained how to appoint someone to make health-care decisions if I became unable to decide for myself. My eyes slowly scanned each intimidating page. As I zeroed in on one part of the form, the part that looked a little like a living will, the language seemed especially disturbing.

Under number four, Statement of Desires, it read:

I want my life to be prolonged and I want life-sustaining treatment to be provided unless I am in a coma that my doctors reasonably believe to be irreversible. Once my doctors have reasonably concluded I am in an irreversible coma, I do not want life-sustaining treatment to be provided or continued.

I nervously bit my lip and read the paragraph again. The column next to it went even further. It talked about withholding or withdrawing life-sustaining procedures altogether. But then I glanced at the next column, which presented a dramatic alternative:

> I want my life to be prolonged to the greatest extent possible without any regard to my condition, the chances I have for recovery or the costs of the procedures.[2]

I squirmed a little in my wheelchair. "Why do I have to sign this section?" I asked. "Can't my husband just privately tell the doctors my views on prolonged treatment?" Ben pointed out that the person whom I would legally select to make health-care decisions for me—if I were unable to make those decisions for myself—needed to faithfully represent my known wishes.

I looked at the place where I would date, sign, and have the form notarized. "What if I change my mind?"

"You should update this every seven years, Joni. Unfortunately," Ben said as he shrugged his shoulders and flipped over the document, "not many people even know about designating a health-care proxy. The few who do, keep putting it off. Then there are those who never take the time to keep the document up to date." He shook his head and paused for a moment. "A lot of headache and heartache could be avoided if people only took time to prepare for the future."

I knew exactly what he meant. I had experienced physical setbacks in 1991 that forced me to think about the way I wanted to approach my own process of dying. I needed to prayerfully and carefully think through health-care decisions, especially if, in the future, I were unable to think.

Questions to Consider

Before I signed my "Joni Tada" on any dotted line, there were serious questions I had to ask. The first was straight out of Psalm 39:4: "Show me, O Lord, my life's end and the number of my days." On one hand, Lord, You say that "length of days" is a blessing, but there has to be a "time to die."[3] This is no decision I can make in a vacuum, it has to involve the Lord and Giver of my life. I need to know what You think about the choices facing me.

It helped that I already had an other-worldly perspective on the process of death. The apostle Paul, who was near death himself, was able to confidently say, "We . . . would prefer to be away from the body and at home with the Lord. So we make it our goal to please him, whether we are at home in the body or away from it."[4] I wanted my decision about the way I would die to meet with His approval, from the last breath I would draw on this side of eternity, to the split-second I crossed the line to the other side.

My decision also involved more than God and me. There were others to consider. For my family's sake it was important to leave an advance directive about the sort of death I wanted to face. Not to sign the document about a health-care proxy could place my husband, Ken, in an awkward position, especially if I were unconscious or mentally incompetent. If a hospital or the state took issue with Ken's directives about my care, then, under the judicial doctrine of "substituted judgment," the court would assume the responsibility of determining my desires regarding medical treatment. Without having documented evidence of my wants and wishes, Ken might end up in a fight with the courts over my almost-dead body.

Also I needed to assess my relationship with Ken, my family, friends, and associates. How would my choices in dying affect them? Would any of my decisions cause intolerable guilt or stress for my husband? And I needed to cement my relationship with my doctor. Did we both appreciate the limitations of my disability? Did I understand all the facts about life-support systems and their help or hindrance to me?

Having thought through these questions and more, I decided to sign the Durable Power of Attorney for Health Care—for my family's sake, for my protection, and for God's commendation.

I took the document home for Ken to study. He knew I had wanted to designate him, and an alternate proxy, as my health-care agents, but we had been putting off the discussion for some time. After dinner, Ken opened the folder on the kitchen table and slowly read each section. He was quiet, and I wondered what he was thinking.

Much later in the evening, he came into the bedroom and sat on the edge of our bed. "This is a good thing to do," he sighed. "A little difficult to talk about but a good thing." He looked straight at me and said, "Well, what have you decided?"

"I know my body better than anybody," I said, "and I know that twenty-five years of paralysis have taken their toll. Let's say, when I'm a little older, I face heart failure, or need to have a kidney removed, or maybe go on dialysis. Quadriplegia has already caused poor circulation and has put my kidneys in jeopardy, so I just don't think it would be worth the risk. I'd probably opt not to have major surgery. Do you see what I mean?"

Ken nodded.

"Plus, I was reading in the Bible the other day about receiving a new body when I get to heaven. That alone makes me not afraid of death," I said. "Like it says, 'And we eagerly await a Savior . . . the Lord Jesus Christ who . . . will transform our lowly bodies so that they will be like his glorious body.'"[5]

"You sound like a walking theology textbook," he said.

"Listen, if you were paralyzed for as long as me, you'd be excited about getting a body that worked, too," I said with a smile. "Anyway, like I mentioned, I'm not afraid of death, but with things so high-tech, and with hospitals so . . . so mechanistic, I'm a little afraid of the way I could die."

"And this is why you want us to sign this," Ken said as he tapped the document in his hand. I nodded, and we both sat there for a long moment. The rest of the evening we spent discussing our wants and wishes of "in sickness and in health, 'til death do us part."

A Living Will Versus a Durable Power of Attorney for Health Care

Why would I designate a health-care proxy? Why not simply sign a living will? At first glance the living will sounds good. You have the chance to write down on paper exactly how "extraordinary" you want extraordinary medical treatment to be. But living wills have problems.

First, such documents send a signal that you don't want to have anything done. For instance, in a crowded emergency room, the overworked doctors on duty could interpret a living will to mean that you do not want to be resuscitated, period. Your stretcher is shoved against a wall while other emergencies waiting in line are ushered in.

Second, a living will cannot be erased at the last minute. You have no idea, when you write it, what sort of death you will face, or what sort of new treatments may become available. There is simply no way you can accurately foresee the details. And who knows, you may, like most people, want to change your mind when faced with the fact of your own death.

People tend to think that a living will gives them control over the way they will die. But in fact, when you sign a living will, you give up rights and control to any doctor who happens to be on the scene to decipher it. There's no guarantee that your favorite, friendly physician will be the one interpreting the vague wording of a living will.

"But," I hear you saying, "can't my family member explain to the doctor what I meant?"

True, family members can take a stab at deciphering what you meant and explaining it to the physicians on the scene, but the doctor doesn't have to heed the advice. The law gives complete power and protection to the physician who has the document in his hands. If it is your own doctor, there may not be a problem; but there's no guarantee that you will be in the same hometown as your family physician when you sustain a serious injury or illness.

So which is it? Living wills or a designated proxy? It boils down to this: Do you want to be represented by a piece of paper or by a person?

I want a person to speak for me. A person, unlike a living will, is flexible and can be responsive to the circumstances. A person can hire or fire a doctor or even discharge a patient from a hospital. But that individual had better know my exact wishes inside and out—my life would be in his hands! Of course, that brings me back to Ken and the Durable Power of Attorney for Health Care. I trust Ken. We share the same beliefs, and he knows me better than anybody. I want him to speak for me.

To be honest, neither living wills nor designated health proxies are perfect answers to the dilemma of dying, but of the two, the power of attorney holds sway. Yet, even appointing a person to make medical-treatment decisions has its built-in problems. Laws vary all over the nation. One state excludes food and fluids from the category of life-sustaining procedures, and other states allow people to decide specifically whether or not they want food and water withheld.

What's the best thing to do? Ask questions. Whether in a family conference with the ethics committee at the hospital, or in a discussion with nurses and social workers, it's always good to ask.

The "Miranda" Law
You Have the Right to . . .

Actually the Patient Self-Determination Act now requires hospitals or nursing homes that receive Medicare or Medicaid funds to explain which documents are recognized in your state, whether living wills or durable powers of attorney. Your rights as a patient are recited to you when you check into a hospital, a kind of detailed briefing like the Miranda warning that law officers give.

So, whether you're going in for major heart surgery or just overnight observation, you will be handed a frank, written reminder of your right to refuse medical care should your condition become hopeless.

The law was originally drafted in response to the emotional and heartbreaking court proceedings over whether or not to withdraw life support, including food and water, from Nancy Cruzan, the young woman left in a comatose state after a terrible accident. The hope is that this Miranda-like law will make it far more likely that such problems will be resolved at the patient's bedside rather than in some distant courtroom. Nancy Cruzan, before her accident, had never written down her wishes about the way she would want to die. That is why there was so much controversy when her feeding tube was removed, not to mention the outrage over a young, disabled woman's being starved to death.

In one sense, the Patient Self-Determination Act is helpful because people need to know the facts. Yet in another sense it is alarming, even frightening. Just having a nurse confront you about living wills and then handing you a sheet spelling out your rights as you check into a hospital can be disconcerting. A question like that could affect your judgment about medical treatment, especially if you're depressed about being hospitalized. You wouldn't have any chance to think, pray, or plan wisely.

However, the Patient Self-Determination Act, for all of its flaws, is an attempt to get people thinking about health-care proxies and living wills *before* illness strikes and rational thinking goes out the window.

So do not wait until you have checked into a hospital. Prayer is the key for preparing yourself and your family for your decision. Ask God to give you the necessary wisdom to make those important choices. Meet with your pastor. Talk with your spouse or parent. Find out from your doctor what directives are legal in your state, or ask your local hospital or senior-citizens center to send you the information. If you wish, you can write to National Right to Life and request their document, "Will to Live." Then when you receive the information, don't put it off.

When You Sign on the Dotted Line

Okay. So I put my signature to a document. What about you?

Remember, a Durable Power of Attorney for Health Care is not only a legal directive, it is a moral directive as well. I advise you to review a couple of key moral issues before predetermining medical treatment.

If you were my personal friend and I knew that you were about to hammer in concrete: "No life supports in case of emergency," I would say, "Wait! What if you only need those life supports for a few days? What if then you'd be fine? Don't risk throwing your life away!" One more thing: If you exercised your right to predetermine "no life supports, including feeding tubes," you most likely would be asking that you be starved to death, a decision for which you are held morally responsible before God.

A Good Death

If anyone ever died "right," it was Kelly, my five-year-old niece. The youngest of three children, she was the typical tomboy on the family farm. Her mother, Linda, a hardworking single parent, had given her children a lot of responsibilities around the house and barn, and Kelly had become a strong, resourceful, and independent little girl.

One day Granddad noticed that Kelly was limping up the dirt road, slightly dragging her foot. My sister Linda took her to the hospital, and doctors discovered an enormous, cancerous brain tumor. We were shocked and stunned. Surgery could only do so much, and within a month she was confined to a wheelchair. After a long hospital stay, the doctors suggested we take Kelly home to die.

Now there were two sets of wheels around the dinner table, my adult size and Kelly's miniature one. The entire family rallied to focus love and attention on Kelly as she grew weaker. Everyone tried to make her as comfortable as possible. As a result, it was amazing to see the change in this little girl—not so much the physical change, but the change in her spirit and attitude. No longer the stiff-lipped "I don't need help, I can do it myself" tomboy, she softened into the sweetest, happiest child we ever knew. She virtually memorized "Goldilocks and the Three Bears," wore out her cousin Kay at playing tea, and most of all, let her imagination run wild when it came to talking about heaven.

Kelly tired easily during those last few months and spent more and more time in bed. She seemed to have no fear of the dark, her disability, or death. One night I remember passing her dark bedroom and hearing her sing in a half-whisper, "Jesus loves me, this I know. . ."

Kelly taught us much about dying right. She talked glowingly of when she would eat ice cream cones with Jesus. She would ride bigger ponies, douse all the ketchup she wanted on her hamburgers, and maybe, like Goldilocks, even talk to bears. At one point when we were alone in her room, I looked at her in all seriousness and asked, "Kelly, when you see Jesus, will you please tell Him that I said 'Hi'? You won't forget?"

She smiled and nodded.

Earlier in the evening on the night Kelly died, she said to her mother, "Mommy, I want to go home."

"But you are home, honey," my sister tenderly told her.

"No, I want to go home with Jesus," she whispered hoarsely. Within several hours she was there. Kelly passed away surrounded in bed by her family, stuffed animals, and a suitcase packed with her jeans, dresses, and toys. Kelly died right, and that fact alone did more to ease the heartache and pain of her passing than anything else.

Hospice Care

Three simple things her family did made Kelly's death good. First, her pain was kept under control and she was made as comfortable as possible. Second, the family was brought together. Kelly gave sisters, cousins, uncles, and grandparents a reason to unite, support, and care for one another. Third, Kelly remained a part of the community. Neighborhood children played board games at her bedside, Granddad endlessly read picture books to her, and harmony rang out as she weakly joined in family sing-alongs. She was in almost constant contact with loving people, who continually convinced her she was not alone or deserted in her time of need.

What happened in Kelly's case is very much what happens in a hospice setting. We practiced most of the principles you would find in an in-patient hospice—that is, a place where people go to die. But a good hospice is not in the business of dying, but of *living* right up to the end. There's nothing institutional about rooms that are filled with homey furniture, throw rugs, and paintings on the walls. You may even see a beagle, someone's family pet, ambling down the hallway.

Modern medicine often handles death very poorly. A hospital will go to great lengths for the sake of a patient with a chance of recovery. But a dying patient who languishes in a bed, a bed that others could be using, is often an embarrassment. Sometimes in a busy, crowded hospital, people who are terminally ill and dying are very much alone.

To me it's unfortunate that so much attention and so many resources in our society are funneled into legalizing euthanasia while the hospice movement is struggling to stay alive. To be honest, in the United States you are unlikely to be offered a bed in a hospice facility since there are very few. In-patient hospices, most of which are run by religious organizations, are in desperate need of volunteers, money, and facilities.

As a result, in this country the emphasis is on in-home hospice, the sort of thing we managed with Kelly. In-home hospice provides a trained nurse for several days or a week to give a stressed-out caregiver a break. Social Security will even pay for some of the expenses of such care. But the movement needs help. We would communicate a far more compassionate message to those who are terminally ill and dying if we focused our energies on helping people die right.

To die right. That's what it is all about. Unfortunately euthanasia has become a popular topic because people are led to believe that death by suicide or homicide is more dignified than dying naturally. True, there can be bad medical treatment administered at the end of a person's life, but there are good treatments, too, exemplified in hospice care. It is the answer to those who fear a death that has been robbed of dignity by bad medical treatment.

We can even help debilitated or terminally ill people live right. We can alleviate the hopelessness that drives debilitated people to despair by advocating attendant or respite care for stressed-out families. We can support the family with counseling, visitation, or financial aid. Living or dying can be a lonely, desperate time for a person who is terminally ill. Our society, especially the spiritual community, cannot cringe at the misery that needs mercy or shun the burden that requires bearing. We must be the Lord's hands and heart to those who hurt.

A Dying Breath

Death, no matter how we plan for it, is still the last outrage. But we can make dying as peaceful and serene as possible. You actually can go through death in peace, even serenity. It all depends on the way you view life.

If you believe that your earthly life will continue uninterrupted, then you will never be prepared for your final passage, no matter how many documents you sign.

If you believe that life has no meaning beyond what you are doing today, then death will be, to you, an ugly intrusion full of bitterness.

If you believe that life is a tiresome struggle weighted with failures and disappointments, then dying, for you, may be a fatal escape.

But if you accept life as a gift from God, then dying is a part of the given. You can prepare for it. You can approach it. Because you can say, "For to me, to live is Christ and to die is gain."[6]

Discussion Guide

Be Prepared

1. Given what you have read in this book and have heard in the media, what steps will you take in the future to be prepared? Why or why not?

   Have a family meeting?

   Write a Living Will?

   Sign a Durable Power of Attorney for Health Care?

   Wait a while to see what happens in the courts?

2. Power of attorney carries with it great responsibility and doesn't always solve the dilemma. Consider the following scenario.

   Mary, a Christian nurse, signed a Durable Power of Attorney for Health Care while attending a seminar about advanced directives. In it, she expressed that she did not want to go on long-term life supports should she become mentally incompetent. Her husband agreed to be her healthcare proxy. Mary, as a result of a serious automobile accident, is now in a coma. Her husband now must make the decision whether or not to withdraw his wife from life supports. Should he or shouldn't he?

3. Not every situation will even have a piece of paper
    providing some kind of direction.

    *George, an adult with Down's syndrome, has been
    attending your church. He has developed many
    friends at church. He lives in a residential facility
    and his legal guardians are distant relatives who re-
    side in another section of town. George has recently
    developed a degenerative hip problem which, if not
    corrected, will result in his inability to walk. The
    director of his residential facility approaches you,
    concerned that George's legal guardians have vehe-
    mently opposed the operation.* To what extent
    should you get involved?

10

LIVING VICTORIOUSLY

To Whom It May Concern:

I hate my life. You can't imagine the ache of wanting to end your life and not being able to because you're a quadriplegic and can't use your hands.

After the doctors did surgery on my neck, I refused to wear a neck collar. I hate it too. Nobody understands and nobody will listen to me when I tell them I don't want to live. People feel sorry for me and I can't stand it. I can't even go to the bathroom by myself.

I don't have the energy to cope, I don't have the strength to face the next day. I want out.

A depressed teenager

What would you say to this teenager? What sort of advice would you give her? Now that you've come this far, I certainly hope you would not give her a copy of *Final Exit*!

It's safe to say you'd want to help. But how much time and support would you be willing to invest in her? It would take a lot of effort to sit by the hospital bedside and listen, to hold her hand, and genuinely care. She might spit abuse at you . . . she might turn her head on the pillow and sullenly ignore you . . . she might even scream at a nurse to kick you out of the room.

Could you, with supernatural love, turn the other cheek? Would you be able to care with no strings attached? Would you think to come back the next day with a *Seventeen* magazine, a package of Twinkies, and just quietly sit at her bedside to watch *Star Trek*?

That girl is one of millions—depressed, disillusioned, and crying out the unspoken question: Where is life that is worth living? Remember, the answer to that question comes not in the form of a sentence but in people.

Finding Answers in People

The suicidal teenager who wrote the "To Whom It May Concern" letter was me. I begged my friend Jackie to bring from home her mother's sleeping pills or her father's razors. I daydreamed of the time when I could sit up in a motorized wheelchair and power it off a high curb (just my luck—I would only become brain-injured and worsen my misery!). When my friend stubbornly refused, I waited at night until no nurses were around so I could thrash my head on the pillow, hoping that my neck would snap at a higher level and cut off my breathing.

I had no pride when it came to bowing out of life. The funny thing is that at one time I had said, "People who cut their lives short are weak-minded, weak-willed wimps who have spaghetti for a backbone. Why can't they pull themselves up by their bootstraps, hold their breath, and just charge through the suffering without a lot of mopey complaining!" You'd be surprised how many people feel that way, at least until they are the ones who become emotional spaghetti.

When a diving accident paralyzed more than just my body, all I wanted was to escape. Escape into daydreams. Escape into sleep. Escape into television. And if I were able, escape into death.

I am not the only one. Millions more don't want to suffer through anything, whether it be bad health, bad finances, bad pain, or bad relationships. Escape has become the great American pastime, and our culture doesn't help. Our media-oriented society tries to sell us one image after another of the good life free of pain. When a society buys into that culture of comfort, it is just a short hop, philosophically, into the hospital or nursing-home lounges, where life-and-death decisions are made. Or it is just a short hop to the local bookstore to pick up a copy of *Final Exit.*

Thankfully, I never was able to engineer that final escape.

Instead I found other answers rather than an escape hatch; those answers came in the form of people who loved me. Mrs. Miller, the mother of a high-school classmate, visited my bedside once a week. I was embarrassed to show anger in front of her, and besides, she brought in home-baked sugar cookies. A boisterous and hardy high-school friend named Diana gave up a semester of college to stick by my bedside. Her commitment impressed me, and I liked her corny jokes. A boy named Steve loved the challenge of answering my questions about the Bible. I tolerated him because he was younger than I.

People like these took away my desperate urge to escape. In fact, I found their company much more satisfying than any escape hatch. Steve, for instance, was so caring and persistent. I'll never forget the time I cornered him and whispered half-crying, "It's so . . . hard."

He didn't say a word but picked up his guitar and sang an Elton John tune, ". . . my gift is my song, and this one's for you." The words of the music contained no answers whatsoever for my despair, but the tender and innocent expression of love on his young face was all the healing I needed, at least for that moment.

Mrs. Miller, Diana, Steve, my sisters . . . these people connected me from one healing moment to the next until I had finally surfaced out of my suicidal despair. I looked back into the fog of that unreal depression and realized that I hadn't found answers so much as I had found friends.

God Understands Too

There's hardly a soul who has ever lived who has not wrestled with the overwhelming urge to escape suffering, permanently. In fact, the strongest most stalwart of saints are sometimes the most likely candidates for ending it all.

Even a powerful prophet like Elijah discovered that he had spaghetti for a backbone. When the wicked queen Jezebel heard through the grapevine that Elijah had wiped out hundreds of her prophets, she went after his neck. Elijah got weak-kneed and ran for his life. When he reached the desert, he gave up. He didn't even have the courage to do himself in—he begged God to perform the mercy killing on him.

"I have had enough, Lord," he said. "Take my life."

Here's a curious footnote. God had used Elijah to perform spectacular miracles just the day before. Elijah had announced the end of a drought. He was the people's best friend. Elijah had nothing to complain about. Why in the world would he, of all people, want such a permanent solution for such a little bit of depression?

That is the point. Whether you are terminally ill and on your last leg, or hunch-shouldered with a bad case of the Monday-morning blues. Whether you are a grandmother facing a dead-end in a nursing home, or a cerebral-palsied young man facing a similar end at the bottom of a bottle of pills—from super-saints to quads like me, no one is immune.

Elijah would understand. More important, God understands. Circumstances may vary from human to human, but we can draw comfort from the fact that all of us are as vulnerable as Elijah. If you look closer at how this mighty prophet surfaced out of his suicidal despair, you will also see that answers came to him in the form of people. Actually, a Person.

God himself ministered to the prophet. God handed him food, maybe even something as tasty as Twinkies. God gave him sleep, and I am sure that Elijah's rest was as quieting and soothing as Steve's gentle song. God even offered a listening, empathetic ear. The record shows that the angel of the Lord touched Elijah and agreed that, ". . .

the journey is too much for you."[1] He then presented Elijah with new work to do. Sometimes, switching focus onto others is just what the doctor would order.

How can I help you see? The lesson of Elijah is for us all. Just as surely as the angel of the Lord personally gave the prophet a sip of cool water and laid him down to rest, the Lord touches our lives through the people He places around us. Mrs. Miller, Steve, Diana, my mother, and my sisters were certainly the hands and heart of God to me. And if there is no Steve or Diana, God can personally come through for you, giving you strength out of nowhere.

Elijah was able to turn the corner and get back on the track, thanks to God. I, too, knew I had turned the corner out of despair when I stopped wrenching my neck on the pillow and started to pray. My prayer during those midnight moments when the faint fragrance of friendship from my sisters, Diana, and the rest was still in the air:

"God, if I can't die . . . show me how to live."

Life Is Worth Living with the Person, Jesus Christ

A prayer like "Show me how to live" assumes that you can see at least a few steps in front of you. But sometimes you can't see a blessed thing. As it says in Isaiah 50:10 (TLB), "If men walk in darkness, without one ray of light . . ."

That pretty much described Dorothy Dalenberg. Total blackness. No way out. Darkness so thick, there was not a single ray of light. Dorothy is not in a coma, does not live in a wheelchair, and is not facing a terminal illness.

But her black and burdensome circumstances are the sort most people can identify with. Maybe even you can:

Dear Joni,

I injured my neck, which resulted in chronic pain and terrible headaches. Suddenly activities I took for granted came at the price of pain, tears, and frustration. Pushing a grocery cart put my neck in spasms. Cleaning the sink left me in bed with pain pills. I was frequently incapacitated, often going to the emergency room for pain shots.

As I fought to cope, my world unraveled. I had sinus surgery, totaled my car, and was told I have fibromyalgia and a glandular disease. God seemed so distant. I could not feel the peace He promised.

I became very depressed. I wasn't living. I was existing from pain pill to pain pill. No hope. So tired. Gradually I decided life was not worth living. I began to think of how I would end it all. I felt my family would be better off without me, but I hung onto their love . . . or maybe their love hung onto me.

I didn't see it at first, but God was there all along. In the friends who listened to me, cared for and accepted me. Through the care of my doctors and a Christian counselor, I learned to control my pain, not let it control me. I discovered my worth is not dependent on what I can do or how I feel. My security comes from who I am in Christ. My life will never be the same. But God has given me a burden to reach out to others in life's dark hours. Pain I will always have, but now I know He will never leave me nor forsake me.

Dorothy Dalenberg

Somewhere in her darkest moment, Dorothy uttered a prayer not unlike mine, "Show me how to live." And Isaiah 50:10 (TLB) was handcrafted for people like her and me: "If men walk in darkness without one ray of light . . ." She felt the thick blackness, and she knew there was not a single ray of light anywhere. Some would say that's a good signal to end it all. But read the rest of the verse: "If men walk in darkness without one ray of light, *let them trust the Lord, let them rely upon their God*" (italics mine).

When Dorothy reached out in the blackness not expecting to find a thing, not even a light switch to shed some hope on her bleak circumstances, she found the hand of Someone right in the midst of her darkest hour. God showed her how to live when He showed her . . . Himself.

You will only find life worth living if you reach out in the darkness to discover the hand of Christ. Maybe that's why Jesus said, "I am the light of the world." Rays of light are first and foremost found in Him.

And listen to what Jesus says not only about light, but life. He says, "Do not worry about your life. I have come that you might have life and have it more abundantly." He also says "I am the resurrection and the life. I am the way and the truth and the life." Even one of His apostles said, "Lord, to whom shall we go? You have the words of eternal life."[2]

Life is intricately and intimately linked with Jesus. In fact, Jesus is life—He said so Himself. So when we look for life worth living, we must look for it not in happy or heartbreaking circumstances, health, or even relationships. Life is in Christ. That's why Dorothy, and countless others I have mentioned, believe that life is worth living. They count the courage and love, friends and smiles, patience and perseverance, poems and music, peace and hope . . . they count all of this "life" that God gives, worth the pain.

His Eye Is on the Sparrow

During one of my bouts with pressure sores, I became acquainted with a number of sparrows that visited our bird feeder. I envied the sparrows and longed to be as they were, carefree and without boundaries, but I was confined to my bed for weeks on end. On a particularly dreary evening, I was reading my Bible and came across the little lecture Jesus gave on sparrows. He was speaking to His disciples about the future, and when He sensed fear rising in their hearts, Jesus reassured them:

> Are not two sparrows sold for a penny? Yet not one of them will fall to the ground apart from the will of your Father. And even the very hairs of your head are all numbered. So don't be afraid; you are worth more than many sparrows.[3]

I glanced at the bird feeder and smiled. I could understand Jesus' noticing an eagle or falcon or hawk falling to the ground. Those are important birds God created, the kind worth attending to. But a scrappy sparrow? They're a dime a dozen. Jesus said so Himself.

Yet from thousands of bird species, the Lord chose the most insignificant, least-noticed, scruffiest bird of all. A pint-sized thing that even dedicated birdwatchers ignore.

That thought alone calmed my fears. I felt significant and noticed. Because if God takes note of each humble sparrow—who they are, where they are, and what they're doing—I know He keeps tabs on me. For my remaining days in bed, every bird that visited the feeder served as a joyful reminder of God's concern for every detail of my life.

My pressure sores eventually healed, and I was restored to an active life. But there will inevitably be days when I'll still face fear. Worries will press in. Doubts will assault. Depression will lay me low. And you don't have to be in a wheelchair to identify.

We both will do well to remember. "Do not be afraid, little flock, for your Father has been pleased to give you the kingdom."[4] If the great God of heaven concerns Himself with a ragtag little sparrow clinging to the bird feeder outside my window, He cares about you.

A Victorious Crisis

I trust our time together has assured you of God's wisdom. If so, you are prepared to turn your crisis into victory. For crises provide each one of us with the opportunity to yield to the will of God. And such yielding conforms us to the image of Christ and works all things together for good. That is why the life and death dilemma need not defeat the Christian. Rather, the dilemma becomes the beachhead of victory, a place where Satan is defeated and God glorified.

The time of celebrating the victory will be sweet. One day our banged-up, bruised bodies won't matter a whole lot. Right now they scream for our undivided attention, but if we place our trust in Christ, they will one day take a backseat. As C. H. Spurgeon says, "At present we wear our bodies on the outside and our souls on the inside. But in heaven, we shall wear our bodies on the inside and our souls on the outside."

> But God will redeem my life from the grave; he will surely take me to himself.
>
> Psalm 49:15

Discussion Guide

Living Well

1. How would you summarize the message of this book?

2. How do you think your church could get involved in the lives of people facing life-and-death dilemmas? Consider what the church could do for the following:

   Someone who is terminally ill

   A family with a loved one in a coma

   A quadriplegic living in a nursing home

   A mom with disabled twins

3. Why do you think some people are slow to get involved? What would keep *you* from trying any of the above ideas you developed?

4. Apart from involvement in the lives of individuals, what do you think is the role of the church in the societal debate on the life-and-death dilemma?

NOTES

Chapter One

1. Luke 18:40.
2. Joni Eareckson with Joe Musser, *Joni* (Grand Rapids: Zondervan, 1976).
3. Colossians 2:2.
4. Daniel 2:21.
5. James 1:5, emphasis added.
6. Psalm 25:12.
7. Proverbs 9:10.
8. James 3:17.
9. Philippians 4:7.
10. Shirley Locker, "It's So Daily" (Walworth, Wis.: Christian League for the Handicapped).

Chapter Two

1. Job 1:21.
2. Ed Bobs, "Saving Life is Not Enough, the Disabled Demand Rights and Choices," *New York Times,* January 31, 1991.
3. Americans with Disabilities Act of 1990.
4. Jocelyn Elders, Testimony before the Senate Committee on the Freedom of Choice Act, March 27 and 28 (Washington D.C.: Committe on Labor and Human Resources).
5. Dr. C. Everett Koop, from Christian Action Council *Action Line,* July 12, 1985.
6. Isaac Asimov, endorsement on the back cover of *Final Exit* by Derek Humphry.
7. Chuck Colson, "It's Not Over, Debbie," *Christianity Today* October 7, 1988: 80.

8. *Webster's New World Dictionary*, Second College Edition (New York: Simon & Schuster, 1982).

Chapter Three

1. Genesis 2:7.
2. James 2:26.
3. Luke 8:55.
4. Luke 23:46.
5. 2 Corinthians 5:6.
6. Romans 8:20.
7. Exodus 4:11.
8. John 9:9.
9. 1 Corinthians 12:22–26.
10. 2 Corinthians 1:4.
11. Isaiah 35.
12. Luke 7:18–22.
13. Luke 14:21, 23.
14. Romans 3:23.
15. Matthew 12:9–11 (italics added).
16. Isaiah 40:6–7.
17. Isaiah 40:8.

Chapter Four

1. Charles M. Coffin, *The Complete Poetry and Selected Prose of John Donne* (New York: Random House, 1952), 441.
2. Romans 14:7.
3. "Euthanasia: Final Exit, Final Excuse," *First Things* (December 1991), 5.
4. "Ten Reasons Why Washington Physicians Oppose Initiative 119," sponsored by Washington Physicians Against 119, P.O. Box 2071, Redmond, Wash. 98073–2071.
5. H. Hillhorst, V. Kragt, and A. Baanders, *Euthanasia in the Hospital*, English Translation, 1983.
6. Derek Humphry, *Final Exit* (Eugene, Ore.: The Hemlock Society, USA, 1991), 62.

Chapter Five

1. Viktor E. Frankl, *Man's Search for Meaning*, 3d ed. (New York: Simon & Schuster, 1984), 75, 116, (italics mine).
2. Idea from James M. Wall, "In the Face of Death: Rights, Choices, Beliefs," *Christian Century,* August 21–28, 1991.
3. "Quadriplegic Petitions Court to Let Him Die.?" news article, 1989.
4. For further insight into Dr. Viktor Frankl's views on God, refer to his book, *The Unconscious God.*
5. Luke 22:44.
6. "Judge Rules Quadriplegic Can End Life at Will," Associated Press, *Kingsport Times-News,* September 7, 1989, sec. 4B.
7. Idea from Erika Schuchardt, *Why Is This Happening to Me?* (Minneapolis: Augsburg Publishing House, 1989).
8. Tens of thousands of physically disabled young adults find themselves trapped in nursing homes. The disability rights movement has fought to liberate them. In states like California, people with disabilities live in their own homes, raise families, attend school, and hold jobs. Their independent and productive living is partly the result of California's In-Home Support Services Program. It provides financial aid for housekeeping and assistance with personal needs. The case of Larry McAfee contains this lesson: Saving people's lives and rehabilitating them is pointless if they are denied the right and the means to control their lives.

Chapter Six

1. Matthew 4:5–6.
2. John 8:44.
3. C. Samuel Storms, *To Love Mercy* (Colorado Springs: NavPress, 1991): 9.
4. Viktor E. Frankl, *Man's Search for Meaning*, 87–88.
5. 2 Corinthians 4:8–10, LB.
6. Matthew 18:8.
7. "Deliverance from Hell," *Hemlock Quarterly,* October, 1991, 5.
8. Psalm 139:14.
9. Jude 6; 2 Peter 2:4. Without referencing Ezekiel 28:11–19, it is universally held among Christians that the Devil is one of the fallen angels mentioned in Jude 6 and 2 Peter 2:4. It's a logical conclusion that the greatest among demons would be Satan.

10. 2 Corinthians 4:3–4.

11. Revelation 20:7–10.

Chapter Seven

1. Peter Kreeft, *Making Sense Out of Suffering* (Ann Arbor, Mich.: Servant Books, 1986), 143. God perfectly loves us no matter what level our spiritual maturity; however, many attest that God reserves special affection for individuals who seek Him and fear Him in the manner of the apostle John or King David, men who enjoyed a "best friend" status with God. My use of Kreeft's quote is to underscore that God is more concerned with who we become rather than what we do; thus, giving each of us, no matter what our functioning ability, the opportunity to please God whatever our vocation.

2. 2 Samuel 1:9–16; 1 Chronicles 10:4, LB.

3. 1 Chronicles 10:4.

4. The real issue in this story is, indeed, not one of mercy killing but of harming the person who is set apart for the Lord's service. David was angry that the Amalekite "destroyed the Lord's anointed." We should certainly have as much respect for the life of a chosen child of God as the Israelites did for their king.

5. Exodus 20:13; Matthew 22:39 (italics mine).

6. Judges 9:54–57; 2 Samuel 1:9–16; 1 Kings 16:15–19; Matthew 27:5.

7. 1 Corinthians 6:19–20.

8. Some evangelicals believe moral principles can be violated when there is a conflict of duties. However, in Scripture it is never right to disobey a command of God, and it is never sinful to do right. For further study on whether or not it is ever right to morally disobey God, see Dr. John Frame's book, *Medical Ethics* (Phillipsburg, N. J.: Presbyterian and Reformed Publishing Company, 1988).

9. Hebrews 2:14–15 LB.

10. 1 Corinthians 15:26.

11. John 10:10 LB.

12. Romans 8:18.

13. Elisabeth Elliot, *Forget Me Not* (Portland, Ore.: Multnomah Press, 1989).

14. Ephesians 3:10 PHILLIPS.

15. Matthew 6:34.

Chapter Eight

1. Proverbs 11:14 KJV.
2. 1 Peter 2:4–10.
3. C. Everett Koop, *The Right to Live, The Right To Die* (Wheaton, Ill.: Tyndale House, 1980), 110.
4. Psalm 42:11.
5. C. Everett Koop, "The Surgeon General on Euthanasia, *Presbyterian Journal*, September 25, 1985, 8.
6. Rita L. Marker, "What's All the Fuss About Tube Feeding?" *New Covenant*, January 1991, 19.
7. "Euthanasia," *Ethical Statement*, Christian Medical and Dental Society (May 3, 1990).
8. "The Nightmare Nears," *Moody Monthly* editorial, January 1992, 8.
9. Callista Gould, "Two Real Life 'Awakenings' Challenge PVS Diagnosis," *National Right to Life News*, January 1992, 34.
10. Matthew 16:17.
11. Luke 1:44.
12. Dr. John M. Frame, personal letter.
13. 2 Corinthians 4:18.

Chapter Nine

1. Glen Davidson, *Living with Dying* (Minneapolis: Augsburg Publishing, 1975).
2. "Durable Power of Attorney for Health Care Decisions" (California Civil Code Sections 2410–2443).
3. Ecclesiastes 3:2.
4. 2 Corinthians 5:8–9.
5. Philippians 3:20–21.
6. Philippians 1:21.

Chapter Ten

1. 1 Kings 19:7–8.
2. Matthew 6:25; John 10:10; John 11:25; John 6:68; John 14:6.
3. Matthew 10:29–31.
4. Luke 12:32.

162- living will

Joni Eareckson Tada is founder of JAF Ministries.
For information on how your church can accelerate
outreach into the disability community, contact:

JAF Ministries
P.O. Box 3333
Agoura Hills, CA 91301